Cake

Cake

A Memoir, Not a Cookbook

Rhonwyn Crownover

CONTENTS

For Winter, for Spring, and for Summer...

"When everyone else is losing their heads,
it is important to keep yours."

- *Marie Antoinette*

There's another famous quote we all
attribute to Marie Antoinette, but I don't see
how that's relevant to this story.

Step 1

Preheat Oven

My First Cake?

**There's an old Polaroid buried in a storage bin at my parents'
house** that I like to consider the first slice of evidence supporting my
introduction to cake. It's a photo of my dad, myself, and Barney the
Purple Dinosaur. My dad's holding me on his hip. This was the early
nineties, so his hair is still a deep espresso, and his skin is tan from his
many Navy days out in the sun. He's wearing white khaki shorts that
reveal two-thirds of his lower thigh and a color-block polo shirt. The
ensemble is completed by wraparound sunglasses with a string tied in
the back, for both security and style.

Dad is grinning toward either me or Barney; it's hard to tell from the
sunglasses.

I'm dressed for the occasion as well; a pale pink dress with white frills
and a matching white sunhat. My white socks are tucked into what only
appear to be red and blue...bowling shoes? It's a far cry from the white
patent leathers you'd typically see for whatever occasion this might have
been (presumably a birthday party, judging by the presence of our
dinosaur friend). But, my parents were poor at the time, so maybe the
hand-me-down bowling shoes were the best they could do.

I'm looking toward Barney. I'm not in tears as you'd expect of a
two-year-old. Instead, my tiny teeth are bared in a grimace, and my head
is leaning back about as far as it can safely extend without toppling me
out of my dad's arms.

I have no memory of when or where exactly this photograph was taken, and I'm writing this without having asked my parents about it, but there are two things I know for certain.

One - This is not my birthday party. For one, Barney is pristine. This is no budget Barney. This Barney looks like he could very well pop onto channel 34 right before this toddler's very eyes and sing along with Baby Bop and all their dinosaur friends. It's also far too sunny of a day to be my party. I was born in October, so we'd be a bit more bundled up, even in Virginia. I don't know whose birthday it was, or where we were, but this was not my party.

Two - More importantly, I ate cake that day. There's no evidence. There are tables surrounding us in the picture, and not one shows the slightest hint of a fork or a paper plate. There's no smudge of chocolate or vanilla on my dress. Nevertheless, I can feel it in the depths of my soul. To this day, twenty-something years later, I know that the toddler in this picture ate cake. You can see it from the satisfaction of her eyes. Sure, she was apprehensive of Barney, and she was almost certainly overstimulated from the events of the party, but you can tell. I look at this photo and I am certain; this toddler ate cake.

Today, I can only speculate on the flavor.

Maybe chocolate. A rich, deep, melt-in-your-mouth kind of chocolate. Baked with an earthy cocoa powder and topped with a chocolate ganache. Add a little strawberry inside to balance out the rich decadence of the cocoa.

There's also the possibility that it was ice cream cake. It was a kid's birthday party after all. It was summertime. Biting into a creamy cold treat surrounded by flaky cake would not be such a bad idea.

Of course, it very well could have been vanilla. It's a true classic. With a pillowy soft crumb, begging you to sink your teeth into its buttery goodness. Layer in some buttercream icing with sprinkles on top to dress it up for the occasion. There you have it. Instant crowd-pleaser.

The flavor is almost certainly lost to history, but I know it in my heart of hearts; I see this Polaroid as a beacon, nay, a LUMEN of hope. It is the earliest slice of evidence that I, Rhonwyn Crownover, have, in fact, eaten Cake.

Cookie Cake

Just like every other sleepover, Danielle decided she needed to call her dad to pick her up from Natasha's birthday party. I thought she'd grown out of it. After all, we were about to be *second graders*. Calling home early is first-grade *baby* stuff. On the other hand, this was Danielle Harvey we were talking about. She was my best friend, but she never even made it a whole night at *my* house! We loved Natasha, but nobody's house was going to make Danielle comfortable enough to stay.

Danielle stayed the length of the actual party of course, and it was a great one. Natasha had a cookie cake from Schnucks.

There was a plastic Barbie, or maybe a princess adorning the top of the cake (I can't remember exactly). The foot of her poofy princess dress read "Happy Birthday Natasha!" in green icing. It clashed against the pink of the princess's dress, but green was her favorite color, after all.

Cookie cakes were Natasha's favorite and for good reason. With cookie cakes, you want to eat something heavy, with chocolate or white chocolate chips sprinkled throughout that erupt in your mouth as you indulge in the crumbly pastry. Some may argue that a cookie cake isn't a cake at all, but like Natasha, I disagree. It serves every purpose of a cake - bringing people together, celebrating one or a few people with its decorations, and sharing sugary goodness with all of the guest-of-honor's friends. That, my friends, is a cake.

Natasha sat and watched her seven candles flicker as we sang Happy Birthday. We all clapped and celebrated with our friend, indulging in our treat while she opened her presents. The best present, Natasha must have deemed, was *Candyland*. The new version with the cuter princess on the front–not like the creepy 1980s one. I don't know who got it for her, but it wasn't me. I'm an awful gift-giver. But that's a story for another chapter.

Natasha propped the board game up on display as she made her way through the rest of the presents. It was clear that a battle in Candyland was imminent.

Crashing from our sugar high, we changed into pajamas and circled around the game in the living room. Our plastic markers were just rounding the corner of *Gumdrop Mountains* when Danielle decided–it was time.

"Rhonwyn," Danielle drew a cupped hand to my ear and whispered, "I want to go home." As best friends, the unspoken code of any sleepover was that I would have to accompany her if she was faced with any reason to talk to grown-ups. For Danielle, there was always a reason.

"It's not even bedtime yet!" I whispered back, acutely aware that my turn in Candyland was coming up after Bree. Bree was only 8 spaces ahead! If I could make it to *Gumdrop Pass* I could pull into second place, and maybe even take the lead before we made it to *Molasses Swamp*.

"Yeah, but I just want to go home," she said. Her voice cracked as she pleaded her case. Restlessly, her gaze darted around the room, desperately searching for a sympathetic adult. Then, the tears started to well up. The diagnosis was clear; Danielle was homesick.

"We have to go to the bathroom," I lied to the other girls.

"We don't wait for skips," said Natasha.

I understood. It was a fairly universal rule. In my seven years, I'd come across it many times. If you leave the board when your turn rolls around, you lose it. Firm, but fair. Still, it was hard to hear that my plans to take the lead may be thwarted by Danielle's chronic homesickness. *Seriously, did it have to be every time?*

I stood up with Danielle, taking one last look at any potential I had to pull forward on the board.

I watched as Natasha's friend, Angie rolled the dice. At least they were all unaware of Danielle's quick exit strategy.

Danielle and I wandered into the kitchen to find the grown-ups. Natasha's mom was starting to wash up dishes.

At the dining table, Natasha's aunt, Ms. Talia was combing through Mia's hair. Mia was Natasha's best friend and in our grade at school. I was surprised to see Mia away from the board game knowing the skip rule. Mia was as competitive as I was, if not more. She was so effortlessly smart. At school, she and I were always battling for the best grades. When the spelling bee came around a few months before and we had to pick a representative for the class, she and I spelled words straight through recess. To my dismay, I lost on the word "nostalgia" and we sent Mia the next week to represent our classroom.

Squeals of joy reverberated through the kitchen walls. The girls in the living room were clearly making some moves. I remembered Mia was in second place before Danielle got up. That meant Bree would have overtaken both of us at Candycane Woods if Mia left earlier than we did. At least we were all in a losing battle together.

Recognizing a window of opportunity in the competition, Mia and I exchanged knowing glances with each other. Still, we kept quiet since Mrs. Young was already dialing.

While Danielle made her phone call, I joined Ms. Talia and Mia at the dining table. I watched as Ms. Talia yanked at Mia's thick hair with a hairbrush, almost dragging the whole girl with it as she tugged.

On the table in front of me, I saw the hair ties Mia always wore. There were three on the table, each decorated with two cubed bobbles at the end. These ones were translucent pink with a bit of sparkle throughout the plastic. The popular Black girls at school would accessorize with them— usually something colorful and translucent for day-to-day use. To be a kid in the 90s meant it was an age of translucent decor, and hair was no exception. Mia always wore pink ones. I thought they made her hair look so gorgeous in her fanciful twists, but looking at the baubles close up in front of me, it made sense that these hair ties wouldn't be comfortable to sleep in.

That explains the hair brushing. I thought. It was different from my home routine where mornings were for hair brushing and night-time I just plopped on the bed when I ran out of steam.

Mrs. Young hung up the phone with Mr. Harvey.

"He said he's on his way, so go ahead and pack up your stuff," Mrs. Young instructed Danielle with a smile.

I stood up to follow Danielle, but Mrs. Young stopped me, crouching down to my eye level before speaking.

"Did you come in here because you want to go home too, sweetie?" she asked in a deep voice, "I know there was a siren outside earlier, and it's okay if you're scared."

"No!" I said confidently, "If I'm sleeping over, I *always* stay over, Danielle just *always* gets scared and calls her dad."

Mrs. Young chuckled warmly, and I hurried after Danielle to help gather her things.

Sure enough, when Danielle and I returned to the board, my tiny green game piece stayed just on the other side of Gumdrop Mountains. Bree was nearing Candy Castle already. She'd win for sure. Natasha had managed to pass me up, making her way nearer to Lollipop Woods. I wanted to pass Gumdrop Mountain before, but now I *needed* it if I had any hope to take second place.

Unfortunately, I hadn't been able to recover from my skipped turn at Candyland by the time Mr. Harvey arrived to get Danielle. The girls all joined us to say our goodbyes. It was mercy, as I would have been *obliterated* if I skipped another turn.

Natasha gave Danielle a big hug goodbye and thanked her again for her present.

"Are you sure you don't want to stay?" asked Mr. Harvey, like he did at every sleepover.

Danielle nodded silently in defeat, and the two of them headed out to the car. I was sad to see my best friend go, especially since it was my first night staying at Natasha's house, but I knew Natasha, Bree, and Mia from school. Bree was even in my Girl Scout troop. I knew I'd be fine if I just followed along.

Mia joined us back in our Candyland game, but this time, Natasha's mom called Natasha and Bree both back to the kitchen. (This was a stroke of luck. Natasha had gotten stuck at *Cotton Candy Corner* for a turn, so getting a skipped turn from both Natasha and Bree for their hair could mean I stood a chance).

I continued playing with Mia and the other girls, but I kept thinking back to Mia getting her hair brushed before bed. I could see the dining room from the play area. Between turns, I watched as Mrs. Young and Ms. Talia brushed out Bree and Natasha's hair. Everyone's house had different rules, but I worried my chance of overtaking any of the other players might depend on whether or not I was able to get my hair done at the same speed they did. Since I was new at getting hair done for bed, if I messed up at all, I might skip a third turn. In other words, I'd be forfeiting any place other than dead last.

As our pieces drew nearer to Candy Castle, another hair swap was made. Bree was still at the table, but Natasha returned and sent her friend, Angie to the dining room to replace her.

I could feel my face reddening underneath. I felt like I was about to be called on in class—if I was next to the dining table, I wasn't sure what I was supposed to do. We didn't do that at my house.

I studied Angie's steps after she was called back to the kitchen. All she did was get their hairbrush from their bag, sit down in front of one of the grownups, and chat while they got their hair brushed. Simple enough. Fortunately, if I was last to go, no one would really be paying attention if I messed up.

Bree returned and sent Tara in behind her. That's it, it meant I was last for hair. If I played my cards and candies right, the game might even be over by the time it was my turn for hair.

Angie returned from the kitchen right after my turn. I stood up immediately. She didn't have to say it, I was the only one left, so I knew I was next. I knew exactly what to do, so maybe, just maybe I could finish before Bree or Natasha made it to Candy Castle.

I walked quickly to my bag and picked up my hairbrush. I was a little embarrassed by the state of the handle—my dog Billy had a habit of stealing my hairbrush and gnawing on it. Little tooth craters bubbled up at the edge. I hoped I wouldn't get in trouble for that, but maybe Mrs. Young wouldn't notice.

By the time I returned, Mrs. Young was already standing up and starting to push both chairs back into place.

Insecurity surged through me and I was frozen to the floor.

Maybe ... she forgot me? I thought, *Or worse, maybe the rule was that you only had to get your hair brushed out if you wore those bauble hair ties.*

Bree cheered from the living room.

Dangit; she won.

We played to second place, so I knew the game would continue, but it wasn't even about the game anymore. I thought I was getting my hair done next, just like the other girls. Mrs. Young didn't seem to have any plans to brush mine.

Why did she forget me? I worried, *was Mrs. Young mad that Danielle went home? And I helped.*

I felt my cheeks prickle with heat. My heart thudded hard against my chest. I hated when I made a grown-up mad—especially at someone else's house. I didn't know how any of this worked.

Water started to gather at the bottom of my eyelids. *Don't cry. Don't cry. Don't cry.* I told myself internally. But also, *what did I do wrong to mess up this hair brushing so badly?*

Mrs. Young broke the silence, "Oh *that's* right, it's your turn Rhonwyn!" she dragged the chair out loudly across the linoleum, "I must have thought I'd done your hair when Danielle was calling home. Sorry, baby, sit down."

What a relief! I exhaled and took my seat across from Tara, tightly blinking the tears back into my eyes. I sat up as straight as Angie had been sitting before. Mrs. Young brushed gently through my straight blonde locks. She took out a comb and parted my hair down the side before securing it into a single low ponytail. Just like she had done for all the other girls.

After Mrs. Young finished with my hair, I hopped off the chair proudly. The game was over before I got back. I knew I had lost, but for once, competition wasn't my priority. I felt *included*.

* * *

I didn't know it then, but Mrs. Young taught me two important lessons at that sleepover:

The first was a lesson in accepting others. Maybe she had intended to brush my hair all along, or maybe she didn't. Either way, when I hopped off the kitchen chair at the Young house, I felt like I *belonged*. I tried to apply it to my life growing up. More often in my future, the situation was reversed. As I would eat lunch with other blonde girls at the table, I'd see someone else who looked or acted differently from the group. Channeling Mrs. Young, I'd ask if they needed their hair brushed in the kitchen (figuratively)... or a slice of cake (literally). I didn't always get it right (I still don't.) But I always tried.

The second was a lesson in accepting myself. I was trying *so hard* to win at Candyland. I was convinced that as long as I did well at the board game, the night would go fine. While I wasn't the type of shy that couldn't speak to a grownup, I was far too shy to communicate how I was feeling. I couldn't ask the other girls what was going on in the kitchen, or, worse, admit that I was feeling overwhelmed. I was fortunate that Mrs. Young solved my problem that night, but as you grow up, that's not always the case. Sometimes you *just have to speak up*. That second lesson was tougher to master. And it took me lots, and lots, and lots of cake to figure out.

A Tale of Two Sheet Cakes

"No WAY, Mom!" I balked at what my mom was holding during our evening walk through Target.It was a rare treat to go out after dinner on a school night, but Danielle's First Communion was coming up that Sunday, so we needed to buy her a gift. Something possessed my mom into selecting a wooden *Precious Moments* figurine with the words "My First Holy Communion" encrypted below the skirt. The figurine held a Rosary in her hands and she was praying.

I pointed down my throat in a gag gesture to solidify my point.

"What's wrong with her?" my mom defended, cradling the wooden figure as if I might have hurt its feelings, "She has brown wavy hair just like Danielle. Isn't she cute?"

"That's SO lame," I protested, "you remember her Pre-K party, don't you?"

I was, of course, referencing Danielle's graduation present from three years before. She was graduating from Kindergarten, so my mom wanted to be on theme. What does *my* mom have us wrap up and bring to a 5-year-old's party? A *dictionary*. A DICTIONARY! I was barely 6 back then, so I didn't realize what we had gotten ourselves into by committing to such a present.

We went to the after party at McDonald's Play-place to celebrate the graduation with cake and presents for Danielle. *Normal* presents.

A babydoll stroller set that, when pushed, would look like the baby doll was kicking her legs. *Café Polly Pocke*t—you know, the one that would make the waitresses spin when you pressed the lever. *Astronaut Barbie*...I repeat, *Astronaut Barbie;* with the red jumpsuit and helmet included!

My present was next. I watched in horror as Danielle ripped into the pink glitter wrapping paper that I'd painstakingly wrapped the day prior. There it was; an Oxford English Dictionary that Mom had picked out. Danielle moved on immediately to something better. My face was as red as *Astronaut Barbie*'s space jumpsuit.

I was *not* making the same mistake again at her First Communion party. Only by the grace of His Holiness Himself did my mom not just suggest we get Danielle a *Bible*.

"Alright then, what do you want to get her?" My mom conceded. Mom swiftly caressed the figurine's hair to bid farewell. She placed the doll back onto the shelf and gently adjusted her rosary so that the next passer-by might be persuaded.

I dragged my mom to the back wall of the store; the *toy* section. I knew *exactly* what to get her; a Mulan doll. Mulan had just come out a few months ago, and my Disney-loving friend would need this addition to her Princess collection. There were two Mulans that year: classic Barbie-adjacent style and action figure style. To follow the collection, we'd have to get her the Barbie style; the one that has her matchmaker outfit and soldier's uniform in the set. It was in stock, and it was perfect.

I placed Mulan into the red cart and we moved on to the wrapping paper. We were blessed to find in the party section a beautiful classic Mickey Ear. Silver with white Mickey silhouettes on the front. Classy Mickey. Understated. (This was a holy event after all.)

There. Perfect present.

* * *

The day came to watch my best friend line up alongside her fellow 7-year-old Sunday School classmates to pledge their lifelong commitment to God. The girls were all dressed in beautiful white dresses lined with lace and ribbon.

Finally, Danielle walked past our pew with her hands clasped together in prayer. She really did look just like that Precious Moments doll mom was hustling at Target. Her wispy hair was curled into a half-up ponytail, tousles falling down her shoulders over her baby-fat cheeks. We did the Catholic thing. Stand. Sit. Kneel. Sit. Kneel. Stand. "Peace Be With You." Sit. Kneel. Body of Christ. Kneel. Stand. Exit.

The afterparty was small; just Danielle's dad, his girlfriend, and grandparents from both sides.

Danielle's mom was coming too, but she was running late. It was typical for her mom to run late, but the unusual part was that she was literally JUST at the church. How can she run late on the same drive everyone else just had to the party?

Not worrying about it further, I made my way to the dining room table to place my silvery-wrapped Mickey box with the rest of the gifts. It had fit in well from the outside. Mostly white, silver, and pastel-colored wrapping paper, just like the others. I was relieved. While dropping my gift off, I looked around for the cake.

Opposite the gift table, the kitchen was filled with fruits, a cookie platter, sodas, and pizza boxes that I expected we'd dig into soon, but there was no cake to be found! No multi-tiered centerpiece with white royal icing. Not even a simple sheet cake! I crinkled my nose in disappointment.

Being the only other kid at the party, I crept upstairs to Danielle's bedroom while she changed out of her white communion dress. While she slipped on her Mickey T-Shirt and a pair of jean shorts, I entertained myself with Ricardo, her pet mouse.

"Hey did your parents not let you get a cake for this?" I asked subtly, "I remember they had cake at Gina's Communion."

"Oh no, no WAY." She replied instantly.

I was taken aback by the tinge of fear in her voice. "Why not?"

"I refuse. You remember what happened at my pre-K graduation!"

"Pre-K Graduation?" I repeated, "I was just talking about that this week when my mom and I were at Target getting your gift." Anxiety drove my fingernail between my teeth as I considered the possibility that Danielle might have been worried about her gifts, and somehow tied it back to the cake. *Was this evidence that our Dictionary ruined her graduation?*

"I promise it's a way better gift," I reassured both Danielle and myself.

"No..." Danielle started. She looked about as anxious as I was feeling. She whipped her head back and forth as though the Bratz dolls on her dresser would judge her for what she was about to say. Finally, in a hushed tone, she confessed, "I cut the cake wrong."

"You cut the cake wrong?" I repeated, louder than she liked.

Danielle flopped down on her twin bed, right on top of where she had laid her communion dress. "I had one of those big square cakes, but I didn't know how to cut it. So I cut a *triangle*. And then everyone laughed."

I couldn't help but laugh at her. "I don't remember that at all! I was too worried about what I got you!"

Danielle was still sulking "I'm never having cake again. I told my dad only cookies from here out."

"You're SO DRAMATIC," I told her.

As if on cue, we heard an "I'm HERE!" – Danielle's mom's voice echoed through the house as the screen door screeched open.

Danielle and I walked out on the balcony to see the former Mrs. Harvey with bags of gifts hanging from her arms. The screen door was held open by her butt, accentuated in size by her high-waisted denim mom jean. Then I noticed what she was holding, I looked at my friend. Danielle's face was pale.

"Oh, hey Munchkin," she said, seeing Danielle at the top of the stairs, "Come here and help me with this cake."

Ms. Harvey was holding a Dairy Queen ice cream cake in her hands. I guessed from the color that it was an Oreo flavor. Condensation from the frozen cake in the warm spring air made it too cloudy to gauge.

"Can you believe your *father* didn't get you a cake for your First Communion?" Danielle's mom said loudly enough for the guests to hear. "I got your back though," she added with a wink.

"Mom, I didn't *want* a cake!" Danielle insisted as the other guests started to gather around to greet Ms. Harvey. "We got cookies instead."

"Oh here, let me grab that for ya," said Rita, walking in from behind us. Rita was Danielle's dad's new girlfriend. She took the cake from Ms. Harvey and brought it into the kitchen.

"I don't want cake, mom." Danielle protested quietly.

"It's your Holy Communion, honey, we have to have a cake. Come on, let's go cut into it and then we can open *presents*!"

Aunts and Uncles gathered around the kitchen table to watch Danielle cut into her cake. Mr. Harvey towered over the rest of the Harveys with his camcorder to record the moment. My parents and I, not being family, took a spot toward the back.

"This one's a circle!" Ms. Harvey called out as Rita handed Danielle a knife. Some of the others laughed quietly, and Danielle's face reddened. I wondered if they actually remembered the snafu or if they were just being polite.

I watched my friend cut a perfect triangle into her Oreo cookie cake. Rita took the first piece and set it on a plate for Danielle. Danielle stepped back as Rita cut into the rest of the pieces.

After waiting for my slice of cake, I sought to find Danielle again. She had made her way to the back of the room.

"See, it wasn't that bad." Always feeling like the big sister, I had to reassure my friend.

I sank my teeth into my slice of ice cream cake.

Oreo Cookie cakes. Beneath the crunchy Oreo crust lies a silky smooth iced treat. The balance of two polarizing textures creates a mouthful of celebration. A children's classic. The best of two desserts.

From what I overheard from my parents' nightly dinner gossip, Ms. Harvey was the wild card in the divorce. She was the Oreo to Mr. Harvey's Ice-Cream Family, but at that moment, as I devoured my slice, I was grateful for her spontaneity.

Next, it was time to open presents. The moment I'd been waiting for the entire day. I followed the crowd into the living room. The piano bench was always the seat of honor at the Harvey House. Danielle took her place in front of the piano and faced outwardly toward the couches so we could all see. Rita and Ms. Harvey carried in the presents.

It was my moment–the time to be vindicated. She opened my present first! (who are we kidding, of *course* she did, aside from *maybe* Jesus, the person she idolized most was Mr. Mouse, and that wrapping paper stood out).

"Congratulations on your Fir- First Comm-Communion" Danielle struggled her way through the rest of the note my Mom had written on the card that morning. Her crossed feet swung on the bottom of the piano bench as we all waited for the thoughts to wrap up. "Love, the Crownovers - Jeannine, George, and Rhonwyn."

Danielle grinned widely as she dove into the present. There she was; Mulan. Only the back of the box was visible from my angle as Danielle inspected the doll and all of her accessories, but my friend was smiling ear to ear.

"Ooh look there's a little Mushu!" she exclaimed. She was happy!

Success! I thought, reveling in her happiness. *Vindication.* My friend and I both made up for our social gaffes at the Pre-K graduation. It was a celebration to remember.

"Okay, we'll play with her later." Rita traded the Mulan doll for an unopened gift wrapped in simple white paper.

Danielle read the next card from her Grandma on her Dad's side. She then tore into the gift. A bible study book for girls. A grandma present to be sure, but that's to be expected at an event like this.

The next gifts came one by one. A holy prayer candle. A Teddy Bear with Angel Wings. A Bible. *A Precious Moments Figurine.*

It was on the last present that I realized–*my mom was right*. This was a holy event. Again, I misjudged the assignment and got the wrong kind of gift! My face reddened at the thought of another gift gaffe.

More presents were opened one by one. A book of prayers. A porcelain angel. My colorful Mulan Doll sprung up through the shards of gift wrap, clashing against the solemnity of the rest of the gifts, and I sunk deeper and deeper into my chair, gnawing at the edges of my fingernails until a prick of blood began to form.

* * *

This was only the beginning. I've recovered from the embarrassment of Danielle's slew of bad gifts (kind of), but I have NEVER gotten gifts right. Unfortunately, each story about cake often ties hand in hand with the presents that accompany that cake. It is safe to assume, if not explicitly stated in each of these stories, that I probably got the wrong gift, and that my nail beds suffered about a week of embarrassment afterward.

To date, Danielle has no memory of the Mulan doll I got her, but that disappointing dictionary has been on her bookshelf for 25 years. Bravo, Mom

Sophie

They would bury Sophie in the dress she wore to her parents'
wedding.

Before, there were four of us. It was always Sophie-and-Gina plus
Danielle-and-Rhonwyn. We were four, but we were also two and two.
This was an age in which, at any given moment, your mom might
say "You can have ONE friend with you when we go to Six Flags." It
was important to distinguish our loyalties. Everyone did. The primary
reason we divided up the way we did was our age gap. Danielle and I
were in third grade while Gina and Sophie were in second. In the classroom, everyone had their best friend by their side, and after school, we'd
get to reunite the pack. It was a perfect foursome. The four of us were
inseparable, but we soon learned that life had other plans.
Danielle moved away to St. Charles after her parents got divorced,
dwindling the crew down to just Sophie-and-Gina plus Rhonwyn.
Trios didn't exist in elementary school. Instead, I was an island. This
was further evidenced by our appearances when Sophie's parents got
married that year.

Sophie was only allowed to bring *one* friend to get ready with the
grown-ups, so I couldn't blame her for choosing Gina. I imagined the
bridesmaids doting on the two second-graders, helping Sophie into her

flower girl dress, and piling Gina's ringlet curls on top of her head with colorful butterfly clips.

I arrived at the church with my family and the rest of the wedding guests. Fortunately, I was allowed to meet up with the girls before the service. My mom knocked on the door labeled "Bridal Party: Debbie Sullivan."

The door pulled inward, and I recognized Gina's shirt-and-skirt combo immediately. After all, it was mine the year before. It was a blue T-shirt and a floor-length floral pencil skirt. Gina accessorized it with strappy kitten heels and the exact butterfly clips I'd expected on the drive there. At just eight years old, Gina already had a talent for turning clothes that once comically hung off of me into something cute–even trendy. It wasn't even just the way Gina looked–the Shirley Temple curls and freckled nose certainly helped–but it was something about the way Gina carried herself that made every girl at Briar Crest Elementary want to be just like her. On more than one occasion, Gina wore a hand-me-down from me one week, and the whole school would wear a copy of it the next. "You're a trendsetter!" my mom assured me the week the whole school dawned Dalmatian-print turtlenecks under their sweaters. "No Mom, *Gina is.*"

Being that this occasion was Sophie's mom's day, even Gina had to take a backseat. If Gina looked like a Mini Maid of Honor that morning, Sophie was the Mini *Bride.* Who knows, if Sophie had lived, that may well have been how it turned out. Sophie wore a beautiful white dress that could have been straight out of a fairy tale. Her blonde curls were tied tight into a classic updo, revealing her perfectly puffed sleeves and a necklace to match her mother's.

I envied the pair's baby fat and intrinsic kid-cuteness, while I, approaching 10, couldn't shed a drop of awkwardness even for a wedding. I had sprouted vertically that year, so my only dress that was wedding-appropriate was a black and white number with a puffed skirt that looked like it was taken straight from a 1987 mail-order catalog.

"There's a phone in the entry room," Sophie said with a mischievous grin – her left grown-up tooth hadn't quite caught up in size to the one on the right, leaving her smile just a bit crooked.

We followed Sophie through the halls of the church like we owned the place. Her dad was the men's Bible Study leader, so she had a backstage pass on a regular day. At her parent's wedding, she ruled the church. We giggled as we gathered around the square table phone.

"Who should we call?" Gina whispered, *loudly* as usual.

"SHHHH" Sophie and I hushed in unison.

"Sorry," she whispered, "who should we call?"

"My brother has a cell phone!" Sophie said. Her older half-brother, Seth was seventeen. He was her dad's son from a previous marriage, but the siblings adored each other, despite the age difference.

We giggled again as Sophie dialed each cubed button. The dial tone stopped and we were connected.

Riiinnggg!

I covered my mouth with a hand to keep in my excitement. Seth would be getting ready for the wedding with the dads right now, and wouldn't know what hit him.

"Hello?" our unexpecting victim walked right into our trap.

Sophie put on a deep voice "UH. Hello, do you drive a red pickup truck?" her eyes widened as we waited for the response.

"Hmmm... I do actually."

"Your pickup truck is blocking the entrance of the church– SHHHH" Sophie covered the receiver to chastise Gina for her hysterical laughter, "... and we need you to move it so the guests can arrive."

"Oh no, is it?" Seth played along, "I better go find my keys so I can move it. Hmm... where did I put them?"

My cheeks burned from the prank we'd pulled off. Seth probably *actually* thought he had to move his car! Just then, as the closest one to the door, I heard footsteps approaching behind us.

"SHHHHH" I told the girls, fearing we'd get caught red-handed. We took deep breaths to suppress our laughs.

"YOU CAN'T FOOL ME!" Seth's voice was sinister and playful as he burst the door open. He was a cool kid through and through, with bleached Ramen-Noodle hair. A suit and tie replaced his normal grunge style.

We all screamed and ran to the other side of the room.

Seth chased after Sophie and lifted her up in his arms. Gina and I laughed and watched the siblings play. A tinge of jealousy shot through me. With no siblings myself, I always envied what Gina and Sophie had; baked-in friends for life.

The wedding was beautiful, of course, and the cake was exquisite. It was a stunning cake adorned with white lace fondant cascading from top to bottom. Atop the cake, instead of the usual figurines, a silvery D and S cake topper added a touch of sparkle. It was a glamorous creation befitting the happy new family.

Butterfly Kisses rang out in the auditorium. It was time for Sophie's mom, the Bride, to dance with her dad. As she took her father's arms, Seth Sr. held out a hand for Sophie.

"And now," the emcee announced, "the bride and groom would like all the fathers and daughters to join them in a father-daughter dance."

Gina and I ran from the kid's table to find our dads sitting together near the back of the room. We joined Sophie on the dance floor. Sophie was barefoot, and her feet rested on her dad's large leather shoes.

I followed suit with my dad through the remainder of the sweet father-daughter song. The music got faster, and all of us girls giggled with each other, twirling and dancing until long after our dads had enough of us and returned to the grown-up tables.

We went back to our table to find the cake was served. We dug into the delicious white cake, which revealed to have a bright red strawberry filling. Refueled with more sugar, we found ourselves running and dancing across the church for the rest of the night.

* * *

Within the year, we got the phone call. It was Mother's Day. Mom was sitting in the living room crocheting her blanket while I fiddled with my dinosaur Tamagotchi pet. Dad was already in the kitchen, so he picked up and stood to the corded phone. My ears perked up as they always did. I couldn't hear what the person on the other side of the phone was saying, but I could tell Dad sounded serious. He put the phone back on the receiver and paused.

Mom stopped crocheting and looked up at him—the way they always did to communicate silently with each other, as if I didn't notice. Something was definitely up.

"Sophie was just in a car accident," Dad said as he marched slowly from the kitchen. "The Prosperis are going to the hospital now…" There was another long pause. "Dana said we should probably join."

We quickly readied ourselves and carpooled to St. John's Children's Hospital, together with the Prosperis. I sat silently next to Gina in the third row of their 9-passenger van. I didn't know what to expect. Even at 9 years old, I could tell the gravity of the situation from the way the adults were acting. I pictured Sophie in a full-body cast like in the movies. With one of her legs up in a sling, and her cast going all the way up over her face.

As we walked through the hallway, the other moms who had already arrived were all gathered around Debbie. She sat in a chair looking at her feet. Mrs. Prosperi and my mom went to join them. Gina and I took a seat in the hallway for what felt like an eternity. Gina wondered if Sophie would have a broken leg, or if she'd even be able to talk. I worried what we would see would be worse.

"We really aren't supposed to let children and non-family inside the ICU," A nurse in Blues Clues scrubs explained to us. Then, softening, "But we can make an exception just this once."

Sophie's room was dimmed. The only light source came from a lamp on the side table. Beeping came from machines to the right of her. Her hair had been shaved on one side, making room for wires to stick to the bald spot. She had some sort of tube running into her nose.

Gina went to her best friend's side first, "Hey Soph, your fingernails are so pretty." She took hold of her best friend's hand, "we're just rooting for you to get well soon, okay."

It was my turn to talk to her. I stepped closer to my friend, noticing more wires across her bare chest. Following the wires up to the screens, I tried to make sense of what each machine was for. I knew the heart monitor one, but there were so many others. It looked like one of the tubes was forcing her chest up and down to breathe, but I couldn't be sure. What I couldn't figure out was how this combination of machines was going to make her better.

"Hold her hand," my mom instructed from behind.

Pink nail polish glittered from Sophie's tiny fingernails. I already heard Gina compliment them, so I didn't know what else I could say. My throat felt heavy.

"Hey..." I finally started, trying to think of a funny memory. I thought maybe a laugh would force her eyes open. That seemed like something that would happen in a book or a movie. If people could hear when they were like that.

Just at that moment, Seth opened the door to the room with his girlfriend. He still had a backpack on, so they must have just arrived.

"Hey sis," he said, stepping next to her bedside and taking her other hand. "Hey, you're gonna pull through, okay? You're tough. You're a Sullivan."

I was frozen to the spot. My friend was hurting so bad she was unconscious and I couldn't think of what to say.

The nurse with the Blues Clues scrubs came back in. "Unfortunately we can really only have 3 guests at a time in here. I'm going to have to ask non-family to leave."

With that cue, the memories flooded back. Summertime trampoline jumping at Gina's house and getting yelled at when more than one of us went on at a time. Walking to the corner store at Sophie's birthday party when her mom let us go to the corner store for candy. Prank phone calls at the wedding.

I couldn't say any of it though, now that her brother was by her side and the nurse was right behind us.

"Say goodbye, honey," the nurse instructed.

I squeezed my friend's hand goodbye for the last time.

* * *

Sophie was buried in the dress she wore to her parents' wedding. Her hair was down this time, brushed in a side part to cover where they had to shave in the ER. She was cradled in a white casket with gold trim.

Standing over the casket, I could tell it was remarkably small; maybe 5 feet from end to end. Too small for a casket to ever be.

There was a satin pocket on the lid that housed several tiny stuffed animals. Gifts that Sophie could take with her while she slept. I pulled the pocket open and added my bright red stuffed puppy to the bunch,

"Take good care of Bridget for me okay?" I asked, finally finding the words.

The gravestone features an etched picture of Sophie smiling ear to ear at the wedding. That left grown-up tooth forever stuck in time. Never quite catching up to the right.

The Journey To The Journey To Bethlehem

I've had an on-again, off-again relationship with God for about as long as I can remember. My family celebrated all the Christian holidays, and I think I'm technically a baptized Lutheran, but that's about the extent of my Christian upbringing. I went through some soul searching after Sophie died–reading what I could understand of the Bible and memorizing the bible chapter names. As an academic overachiever, memorization seemed like the most logical form of piety. However, I found myself worrying more about the state of decomposition on Sophie's body rather than whether or not her spirit was watching me from a fluffy cloud in Heaven. I wanted to believe, but something always broke the relationship.

Growing up, Christmas was always when I felt closest to God. For one, it knocks the other holidays out of the park. The warm plaids, the cinnamon smell wafting through the house, that pillow with a red pickup truck with a Christmas tree strapped to the top (you know the one), and, during my childhood years, Grace Christian Church's Production of *The Journey to Bethlehem*.

For the annual *Journey to Bethlehem*, the whole church campus converts itself into the River Jordan on a journey just like Mary and Joseph took from Galilee to Bethlehem. In my elementary school years, it was a wholesome retelling of the story of Jesus's birth. But there was one year in particular that the Holy Spirit just...left.

Danielle, Gina, and I sat shoulder-to-shoulder on the asphalt in the line to the *Journey To Bethlehem*. This line put Disney World to shame. Like every year, it was at least 3 times the length of the *Journey to Bethlehem* itself. (That is, it's about 3 times the length of the Church's production, not Mary and Joseph's *actual* journey to *actual* Bethlehem; that surely took weeks.) The entire line stretched outside of the Church atrium doors, wrapped around the building, and overflowed out into the neighboring parking lot at Barnwell Middle.

This line, or as I dubbed it years prior, "The Journey to The Journey to Bethlehem," is about the worst sampling of humanity you can find in the Midwest. Imagine, militant upper-middle-class church-goers bundled up for frigid midwest weather on their way to see newborn Baby Jesus, only to be told the wait is upwards of *four hours* on the Friday before Christmas?! What could go wrong?

The sun was long-set, and I was about one-quarter of the way through a well-pointed candy cane. With that in mind, I'd venture to guess we'd just crossed over from Barnwell's parking lot into Grace Church's, but we hadn't quite started snaking through the actual queue posts.

Peppermint flooded through my mouth, chilling my already-cold lips even further. I was trying hard to resist the temptation to bite into my treat (lacking any sense of self-discipline, I have an annual tradition to try to make it through a candy cane without biting into it as though it's some sort of symbolic exercise to increase my patience. I never win). As I sucked away, vaguely listening to my friends talk, I noticed a family of five walking up from behind us. The dad carried a sleepy toddler while two elementary-aged kids followed behind.

Then, the family just *took* a place in line. *Took it!* Blatantly cutting the 70 or 80 people behind them. They didn't even join another family, they just walked right up and decided on a shorter line to start from. I took the candy cane out of my mouth so it was free to gape. Did these people really think their Great Christian Pilgrimage was more time-sensitive than everyone else's?

"Did they just cut?" Danielle asked the rest of us. After exchanging looks of shock, we all stood up. By 11 and 12, we were solidly in middle school, but cutting was a serious offense when committed by an adult. A whole family even!

A man a few families ahead of us spoke up "Hey the line's back there, Buddy!" he said, throwing his thumb behind him.

The family ignored the man, they instead stared straight ahead in the line. The father bounced the baby up and down a few times.

"Hey, Lady!" Gina's Dad bellowed to no avail. "Unbelievable," he added privately to our group.

Our fellow line-cutting victims groaned somewhat in unison. Anger bubbled up inside of me because of this family's disregard for the rules. I crunched into my candy cane. *That's another 20 minutes added to our line.*

"Fucking courtesy! my dad, always having to have the last word, grumbled what we were all thinking. He repeated, "Some people just have no *fucking* courtesy."

* * *

It was probably 9:15 when we finally made it inside the atrium. Our line jumpers from earlier made it on the tour ahead of us, pushing us back a good 15 minutes when all was said and done. It was rude, but we were in no great danger of being kicked out. they would continue to run tours through until midnight.

A boy in his late teens approached us. He was dressed in a tan-colored robe with a gold tassel around his waist. He greeted us and handed everyone a slip of paper.

"Good evening my *Family*. Please, come in, gather, get warm." The boy was theatrical, emphasizing his words at every opportunity, "You have a long journey ahead with our dear Patriarch, *Aram.* We must return to Bethlehem, *and quickly*–there will be *many Roman soldiers* on our journey, and we won't want *trouble.*"

I uncrumpled the slip of paper that I must have subconsciously crushed while listening to the boy's introduction. *Please be Ruth, please be Ruth.* I'd gotten Ruth last year, and quite liked the monicker.

Name: Yael, *Daughter of Lois*
Patriarch: Aram

"Yael?" I repeated, disappointed. I whispered to Danielle. "What name do you have? I'll trade you."

Danielle showed me her paper;

Name: Susannah, Daughter of Esther
Patriarch: Aram

"No fair, you have a normal name in real life!" I half-joked. The name Rhonwyn was always a difficulty on the playground, it seemed only fair I have a pretty name for the evening.

"Yeah... I'm keeping Susannah," said Danielle.

"Ew, yours is awful!" Gina added, reading the paper from over my shoulder.

"I KNOW" my eyes rolled up nearly inside my brain to accentuate my disappointment, "I'm just gonna say I'm Ruth, Daughter of Yael. I'm sure they have that somewhere."

We followed our parents through the hallways of the Megachurch in search of our Patriarch, Aram. Aram was played by a man who looked to be in his late 40s. He had a scraggly beard, no doubt grown for the event, and a big beer belly. He was holding up a sign that read *"Family Aram"* so that our tour group knew where to gather.

As we all congregated, our new dad, Aram began to explain why we must all travel the road from Nazareth to Bethlehem to register our male lineage with the Roman Census.

Aram gestured broadly, acting as if his Oscar Nomination depended on it "...As our family descended from King David, we must register for taxes. Our distant cousin Joseph is traveling with his pregnant wife Mary, and we hope to catch up with them. Mary became pregnant not by Joseph, but by the seed of the Lord our God..."

This was the first time I'd actually listened to the reason for the Journey. The year before, we went to my Grandma's house for Christmas, so we missed Journey to Bethlehem. Before that, I was 10, so I only understood so much. For some reason, I had thought that Mary and Joseph were fleeing from the Romans. I was disappointed to learn from the way Aram was talking, it was more like we were on a journey to the DMV to renew our plates. Ah, well...

When our whole "family" was accounted for, Aram opened the doors to the backyard of the church and the real production began.

Actors, mostly high school kids who were members of the Megachurch congregation, marched through the church grounds – some were dressed in Roman garb, holding torches to light the way as we progressed through the story.

As we walked further along the church sidewalk into the neighboring Ladue Park, Aram explained that the route we were taking was along the roads of the flatlands, parallel to the River Jordan. "We may not know for certain the route our cousins Joseph and Mary have taken," he explained, "but they will almost certainly stop in Jerusalem before finishing their trip. We too will stop in the Markets of Jerusalem to replenish our packs, and rest our heads."

We stopped at a playground. On the other side, huddled around a campfire, were six or seven actors in robes. One was softly strumming on a ukulele, which I imagine was supposed to be a stand-in for a middle eastern *oud*.

"Good evening, brothers and sisters." Aram greeted us.

Before the group around the fire had a chance to return the greeting with a scripted response, I heard giggling boys from behind us. "Good evening *fuckers*" one whispered loudly as the other one laughed. It was too dark to see who the perpetrators were, but I shot a glare back in the general direction of the voices.

Without missing a beat, Aram gestured broadly, ignoring the boys, and bringing our attention back to the script.

"We have traveled from Nazareth in Galilee on our way to Bethlehem. You have not perchance seen a young couple. A woman with child?"

"You do not speak of the Virgin Mary, do you?" said a man from the campfire "The one who is with child, due to bear our King?"

"Indeed, I do, Cousin. Mary and her Husband Joseph. We must find them to celebrate the birth of our savior!"

"I am sorry but I have not seen the couple," said a robed actor I recognized from somewhere. He must have been a sibling of one of my classmates, "however we too are headed to Bethlehem to celebrate and rejoice the birth of our savior!"

"Ah well, we give thanks for your guidance and the warmth of your fire. We must depart. God be with you."

"*Fucks* be with you" the boy in our group interrupted again. Our parents were too far ahead to hear the pranksters.

Gina turned around with a curt "SHHH."

It did nothing but make the boys laugh.

As our friends around the fire faded into the distance, I heard the tour guide of the group behind us. "Good evening brothers and sisters…" He started.

We looped back through the other side of the park, approaching the hill that oversees the parking lot and the sad saps still in line for their tour. The line was getting smaller. It looks like they must have cut it off to make sure they'd be through the guests by midnight.

"Hey, Pops!" My dad said from somewhere in the crowd, "What do you reckon those strange shiny carriages down the hill to be?"

The group let out a genuine chuckle. *This is an example of how and when to be funny on a tour.* I thought, *unlike these boys who ruined the production by saying swears under their breath when the grown-ups weren't paying attention.* Don't get me wrong, my dad was an ex-sailor and swore like one, but he was always in full-dad-joke mode when out in public. Timing and appropriate humor.

Aram laughed politely at the Dad Joke. "Ah, son, I do not believe I've seen such carriages. Perhaps they are a new Roman technology." Aram's dad-joke game was strong. He must have been a dad too.

The group laughed again, but their combined laughter was overshadowed by my dad's baritone "Ha-ha, Excellent!" I smiled at his ability to charm a crowd. I've never had that showmanship, but he always pulled it off so confidently. Dad managed to upstage the boys enough to shut them up for the rest of the tour.

Our trek continued back toward the church to the side entrance hall. The rest of the year, this was where Grace hosted receptions, but in December, it was *Jerusalem*. Two acne-speckled teenagers dressed as Roman Guards swung open the doors to reveal the *pièce de résistance* of the whole show.

The hall was completely transformed into a sprawling indoor market representative of the Jerusalem streets. My exposed cheeks and nose stung as the feeling of modern heating thawed my skin. I took in the sites - the dim lights really lend some realism to the fake brick wallpaper lining the entire hall. Shop owners shouted at us from each side of the market, enticing us to buy their beans and barley.

From the crowd, I guessed there were about three other tour groups in the Market already.

"The Family of Peter!" a voice boomed from behind. Other attendees bundled in modern clothing started to make their way to the side exit of the Market. It became clear to me then that the Market acted as a holding space between the park tour and the visit to the barn to see Jesus, Mary, and Joseph.

"Alas, we are but a poor and humble family, we cannot afford to purchase gifts today for our newborn King. But please, warm yourselves in the market, and speak with the shop owners. We will depart shortly to greet the holy infant." With that, Aram connected with the other tour leaders, presumably to check on how long it would be before we would visit the Manger.

What I can only guess were the two boys from earlier shoved past the crowd in their bowl-cut haircuts, running around yelling "Fuck!" "Shit!" and "Asshole!" whenever they got the chance. *Where were their parents?*

My friends and I separated from our families and explored the shops. Each one had a bit–either talking about their love for the Roman government or secretly telling us the wonders that would await once the baby Jesus came of age.

"The Family of Aram!" We heard Aram's voice from where Peter corralled his tour about 15 minutes earlier.

We made our way to the side exit of the Market. One of the shop owners handed out battery-operated candles for each of us to hold. Some were already turned on from the previous tour group, but I had to turn mine upside down to flip on the switch.

After a brief headcount, Aram led us outside. Blistering cold poured through the doors. After just 15 or so minutes inside, it made the cold nearly unbearable. I can't believe we were out there for upwards of 2 hours in the combined journey and line-waiting.

A little girl of about 6 or 7 started to cry. She had been walking most of the journey with us and was at her limit. She lifted her hands up to her mom to be held, but her mom just shushed her and held her hand.

Sobs broke the girl's speech *"Ii-i wanna go-o ho-ome"*

In sudden escalation, her mom knelt down to eye level, *"I did not stand in this Goddamn line for two and a half hours just so you could throw a tantrum. We're going to see Holy Baby Jesus tonight. You won't ruin this for us!"*

The little girl shut up completely after her mom's scolding. So did the rest of the tour.

Finally, we'd reached the front of the church where the Manger displayed out toward the street. I recognized Kathryn Hamby and Kyle Peters, who portrayed the holy couple. Kathryn was friends with Gina's older brother, Nick. Kathryn and Kyle had been dating in real life since they were in middle school. They were always the leads in the school plays, so it made sense they'd be the leads here as well.

Kathryn solemnly cradled a baby doll in her arms singing a lullaby while Kyle looked on at his wife and child. The three Wisemen presented the newborn baby Jesus with Gold, Frankincense, and Mirr. After thanking the wise men for their gifts, Joseph greeted us.

"Hello, cousins. I am *delighted* to see you've made it safely through your travels," said Kyle, or–Joseph, rather.

Aram nodded, "My dear Cousin, I am so grateful to see you and your growing family. We are but a humble family and have no gifts to present you, but I hope you will join us in song as we rejoice at the birth of the Newborn King."

Mary and Joseph nodded, and we all sang *Silent Night* together while holding our candles.

When the song was finished, we returned our candles to the basket and followed Aram to the main entrance to the church. Coming full circle, we could see that the once-immeasurable line had condensed to maybe two or three remaining tours. I wondered if we would be Aram's last family of the evening or if he had to prep for another circle across Nazareth.

* * *

The final stop of our tour was inside a second hall in the church. We were back in the modern era, under fluorescent lighting. They were holding a bake sale and serving complimentary hot cocoa.

"Can we get some cupcakes?" I asked my mom.

"Oh sure," she said. She was gently blowing on her styrofoam cup of cocoa. She reached into her pocket and handed me a $5 bill. "Get me one too. Whatever looks good."

Gina and Danielle asked their parents for cash too, and we ran to the bake table to buy our treats.

Homemade Christmas cupcakes lined the table.

Holidays mean a festival of confections. Mini Santa's Belts on white cake. Christmas trees on chocolate cupcakes. After the hustle and bustle, delight in the magic of the season with an assortment of Christmas cupcakes! Gingerbread. Peppermint. Each bite is a festive journey, featuring whimsical Christmas flavors.

Gina eyed a giant chocolate brownie. I settled on a white angel cupcake decorated with a North Star on top and got my mom the Santa cupcake. Danielle chose an assortment of cookies for herself. As the old lady behind the card table handed us our cupcakes, a sad-looking teenager handed us a trifold pamphlet. I wondered if she was disappointed to be in the bake sale rather than the Journey to Bethlehem production.

The pamphlet was titled "Purity" and explained all about the importance of remaining abstinent until marriage. I wondered if Mary and Joseph got the memo before the production. (Gina's brother said Kyle and Kathryn went all the way a *year* ago.)

I hoped that thumbing through a Purity pamphlet in the corner of Grace Christian Church would fill some kind of void. I always wanted to believe in God. Some people clearly had faith. The teenagers went all in on this production. So did Aram, the middle-aged man who spent his winters touring proudly through Bethlehem. But between line-cutting, swearing boys, and scowling moms, I just couldn't see how God was around anymore. It just all seemed so hypocritical. Maybe He was around back in the days of Mary and Joseph, but that final year in St. Louis dashed any hopes I had of a creator above.

Do Good, or "Fucking Courtesy" as my dad would call it–that became my faith.

Though I have to admit, sometimes I miss the spirit of the Church, especially around the holidays. And of course, when my kid is old enough, we're *definitely* going to see Grace Christian's *Journey to Bethlehem* production. Or maybe we'll just watch it online. I heard they have a TikTok now.

Red Velvet

Warm desert air breezed through the upstairs office as I Googled furiously on the family computer. Arizona's sun is a heat lamp. Unlike those Missouri summers where the humidity just retains heat all night long, in Arizona, as soon as you approach the wee hours of the morning, the dry air can actually feel refreshing. It can't be defined as cool by any stretch, but refreshing nonetheless. I inhaled the scent of dust and the palo verde tree in my neighbor's backyard. The odd combination calmed my nervous stomach.

It had to be about 12:30 AM as I typed "*Quinceniera*" into the keyboard. At school that day, Valerie Molina had asked me to be a *dama* in her *Quinceniera* coming up that fall.

You see, Valerie's cousin was supposed to fly in from Texas for the occasion but had to cancel. Valerie explained since we had become such good friends in the short time I'd lived there, she was happy for me to join her court.

Context told me this was a huge deal. Of course, I agreed immediately. If nothing else, the request confirmed that I had made my *first* good friend at my new school.

Just like me, Valerie was starting freshman year in high school that August, but she was a whole calendar year older than me. She would turn 15 a week before I turned 14. In Missouri, I was young for my grade, but in Arizona, where most districts do year-round school, I was *The Youngest*. By a long shot. So yes, I was acutely aware that I was about to be the *youngest* person, not just in my grade, but in the entire population of Hamilton High School once the semester started. I needed friends fast if I expected to survive.

To clarify, not everything was transactional here. Valerie had become my friend too! But, a perk is a perk is a perk.

As I waited for the computer to load my results, I mocked my response to Valerie from earlier in the afternoon.

"Of course! I'm so *honored* you asked." I mouthed to myself, putting an emphasis on *'honored.' Why would I say that?*

The memory of her response echoed through the office. "we'll start dance lessons every weekend until the big day! I'll write down the info."

"Did you mean **Quinceañera?***"* my computer finally prompted.
I clicked the link.

Photos of beautiful Latina girls in ornate ball gowns crossed the carousel on my screen. I scanned through the articles.

About The Quinceañera Tradition
The history of The Quinceañera–a Hispanic tradition of one's societal debut, and official entrance into womanhood...

Quinceañera: A Rite of Passage
Are you about to start planning your Quince? Follow our step-by-step guidelines to plan the modern Quince of your dreams!...

More than Your 15th Birthday - A Waltz into Womanhood

> *Join our forum! Prepare for your celebration. Name your padrinos, madrinas, and select your court, all while joining our community...*

> **Quinceañera | WIKIPEDIA**
> *With cultural roots in Mexico and Southern Europe, a Quinceañera is a celebration of a young girl's 15th birthday. The Quinceañera is regarded in many Hispanic cultures as a woman's...*

Wikipedia. There we go. I read through my duties as a dama on Valerie's court. Valerie would dance with her dad, then, when Roberto would take over, the court would follow in and dance the waltz in front of the guests.

There it was; The reason for the weekly dance lessons. I stared at the screen in front of me, feeling my skin percolating with blood at the thought of dancing in front of the whole grade. In 8th grade, I was the new kid. In 9th grade, I would be the freshman who couldn't dance at Valerie Molina's Quinceañera. I was sure of it—somehow, I knew that the most embarrassing moment of my entire life was on the horizon. My stomach lurched again. I'd felt it earlier that day when Valerie asked me originally and I mispronounced "Quinceanera" back to her. My anxiety was getting so out of control that it was PHYSICALLY stabbing me.

I clicked back to my other open tab; Valerie's MySpace page. At the start of the summer, I had altered the HTML for her. She wanted the standard MySpace pink glitter profile template to include a Polaroid picture of Hilary Duff in *The Cinderella Story*. It was an easy enough task—Just copy the pink glitter template, but throw on a link to *The Cinderella Story* Image in the background code.

I wondered if the reason for the background was that it was inspiring her upcoming outfit. Hopefully, my dama role didn't mean I'd be in pink too. Pink wasn't necessarily "me," but the outfit was secondary to the thought of dancing in front of a crowd.

I scrolled down to double-check that I'd had the Polaroids lined up properly below the fold of her profile–an odd HTML mistake that I'd made on Danielle's page.

That's when I saw it; I was Valerie's #6! *Already?!* I'd only known Valerie for a few months. I would have expected #8, if I showed up in the Top 8 at all. Inspecting her page, I guessed that the other five profiles preceding me were the other five damas in her court. It would make sense that she'd want everyone involved in her top 8. Even so, I appreciated the gesture.

I quickly flipped back to the tab with my profile. It was customary to reciprocate any top 8 listings with a comparable ranking, so I knew I would have to move Valerie up to ... I paused.

Up to what? I mouthed, staring deeper into the screen. This was an important decision, and at that point, I didn't have a single Arizonan in my top 8. I'd been coasting on being a "new kid" so it made sense to have strangers on my profile. I gnawed at my cuticle as I began to audit my friendships.

Danielle was certainly staying at #1–I'd known her since I was 3 years old, and even after moving six states away, she would always be number one. No brainer. I didn't have a boyfriend, Gina should have probably been next, but her parents didn't let her have MySpace, so I had Natasha in the #2 spot. I clicked on Natasha's profile.

"I'M NUMBER 7?!" I blurted aloud, forgetting the whole house was asleep. I drew my hand to my mouth to quiet my reaction. How quickly people forget you when you move away.

I switched back to my tab to move Valerie in front of Natasha. It was a generous move on my part to move her up to #2 but, realistically, she *was* my best friend in Arizona. It would be years before I expected to see any of my Missouri friends again, and frankly, I was sitting in the bottom four of almost everyone else's profiles. I had to make a move if I wanted any friends in this new state.

Save. I shut my eyes and clicked the blue button. I was officially entering the MySpace game at Hamilton High School.

This Quinceañera thing is going to be good, I reassured myself. *I have friends now, so it'll be good, as long as I don't fuck up the dancing part, make myself a laughingstock of the entire school, and lose all my friends.*

So no pressure then.

* * *

Day one of dance rehearsals was that Saturday. It was unseasonably cool at just 94 degrees, so I put on my favorite striped polo shirt and dark wash capri pants; I'd only allow my knobby knees and scrawny legs to show around classmates if it was over 110 and I was literally about to die from heat stroke. Capri fashion was a blessing.

When I got inside, Valerie's mom and much older sister were hovering over a huge blue plastic bowl. They had latex gloves on and were massaging some kind of dough concoction that was spicy enough to make my eyes burn. Years later, I learned this is the technique you use to make the very best tamales in the state of Arizona–perhaps the world.

The boys were already in the backyard talking to Valerie's dad. The girls were gathered in the living room admiring a porcelain doll.

"Oh wow, is that your last doll?" I asked while greeting Valerie with a friendly side hug. My Googling had paid off, and my worldly question would make up for my mispronunciation gaffe of the previous week.

"It is! We just picked her up today. Isn't she beautiful?" Valerie beamed at the tiny princess. "Her dress is a bit darker than mine, but otherwise, she's identical!"

Valerie made her introductions as I admired the doll with the rest of the girls. The doll really was beautiful. She had a modern look about her, with hair parted diagonally across the side, and black ringlet curls tumbling out of her gold tiara. She was dressed in a strapless pink ball gown decorated with white and gold embroidery around the bodice. She looked like a colorful pink bride.

"I love her!" Valerie's cousin, Sally gushed, "Is that how you're doing your hair?"

"Thank you! Yes! I had her made to match my hair. Also, look, her nails are painted white instead of pink like mine will be." Valerie added, delicately pulling the ball gown away from the doll's tiny hands, "But I think she'll do perfectly."

A few of the girls sighed in admiration.

"You're going to look gorgeous," Sally reassured her cousin.

As I joined the girls in gushing over Valerie's last doll, I thought of the stuffed animals sitting back in my room that I'd just unpacked and displayed neatly on my dresser. Not being Hispanic, I wouldn't have a ceremonial "last" doll, but until that point, I'd never thought of which one would be my "last." Sure, I didn't play with them as I had when I was 7 or 8, but they were always a comfort. The summer before, I'd even gone through the process of assigning each stuffed animal a "moving buddy" as I packed them into a refrigerator box. My face reddened at the thought of these girls ever finding that only months ago I was re-assuring my stuffed dog Henry that he would in fact be moving buddies with Lamb again. Meanwhile, Valerie was here receiving the symbolic end-of-toys.

The screen door opened and Valerie's dad bellowed from the back-yard. *"Mija! You and your friends get your heels on now. Practiquemos el vals. ANDELE, QUICKLY!"*

As the rest of the girls started to move toward the backyard, Valerie stopped me "Oh right, you don't have heels yet. My cousin is a size 9, and I have her heels here. She glanced at my feet. "Maybe they'll fit?"

I took the shoe box from her, "size seven," I said.

"Oh yikes, well, you're dancing with Carlos and he's probably going to step on your feet anyway, so best to have some padding?" She smiled and hurried me along to introduce me to my dancing partner. I assumed the shoes were going to have to do.

"Carlito, this is my friend Rhonwyn. You're going to be dancing with her now since Patricia can't make it."

As I took in the sight of the backyard furniture spread out to make room for a makeshift dance floor, I felt it again, that deep surge of pain in my lower abdomen. I felt like I was going to shit myself and throw up at the same time.

Oh god, I thought, *we're really going to do this, Rhonwyn. We're going to make fools of ourselves and our lack of rhythm in too-big shoes.*

Valerie's dad taught us all the waltz moves we needed to know. Box Step, Viennese, American, and others I couldn't remember the name of.

Narrations from Valerie's dad drowned out the music almost entirely; "And Glide, Step, Sweep, Together. And Backward, Step, don't-put-your-foot-down-Carlos, Together. Glide, Step, Sweep, Together..." and so on.

Carlos was bad enough at dancing, I found myself slightly grateful that I wasn't the one drawing attention to our hobble. At least Carlos had the directions called out accurately for him. I had to remember that when Valerie's dad said "Backward," he actually meant *Forward* for the girls.

After enduring about an hour and a half of box steps, we all headed inside for much-needed water. We were drenched in sweat. Most of the boys left immediately to shower at their respective homes, doing the world's noses an *immeasurable* favor. The girls stayed behind and gathered in Valerie's room.

"Ugh, I'm so *crampy* today," said Sally, falling dramatically onto Valerie's bed. "I kept messing Manuel up because I am feeling so miserable," Sally added something in Spanish that I didn't understand, and Valerie returned with a lavender rice sock.

Sally took the sock gratefully and pulled up her shirt. Her smooth brown stomach was accentuated by a sparkling butterfly piercing. She applied the sock below the butterfly. I couldn't help but admire Sally's perfect hourglass figure as she writhed on the bed in agony. She had a beautiful body, far from the gangly skin and bones that I was.

"I feel you, girl, I just started mine on Thursday," added Mariah, Valerie's friend from a neighboring middle school.

I learned that Mariah would be attending Hamilton High with Valerie and me when the school year started back up.

Mariah continued, "The last thing I wanted to do today was dance. Sorry, Valerie."

I felt my face redden for about the seventh time that afternoon.

Periods. I knew what a period was from health class. I also knew that you're supposed to start it sometime between 9 and 13. Symptoms include cramping in the lower abdomen, mood swings, appetite changes, and so on. Yet there I was - *an absolute child* by comparison. I was still waiting on my first period, and my 14th birthday was fast approaching.

For the next eight weeks, we practiced our routine until we knew it like the back of our hands. Carlos and I were the third couple to enter the dance floor, followed by Sally and Matt, Mariah and Manuel, and Valerie with her dad. We waltz circles around Valerie until the 3rd chorus, where we move to the side. At this point, Valerie's boyfriend, Evan, came in to escort her as her *chambelain.* We all join in the dancing again until the end of the song. We bow deeply, and the music switches to the second song. At this point, we try to encourage the rest of the guests to join us on the dance floor. For this part in practice, Carlos and Manuel would run inside and scoop up Valerie's mom and Aunt.

It was a lot to remember, but I was getting pretty good. I wasn't half bad at dancing once there was a routine to memorize.

Ninth grade had started at some point during the weeks of practices, and I was feeling a sense of belonging–these were my friends. At lunch, I joined Valerie and Mariah at the outside tables. We would talk about Valerie's upcoming Quince, general school drama, and complain about teachers. Even Sally, who was a Junior, would wave hello to me in the hallways.

* * *

The morning in September finally came. Valerie's big day! I curled my hair and pinned it up on two sides–my hair was too short to be in an updo as Valerie had requested of her damas, but I tried to be respectful with the clips. I slipped on the spaghetti-strapped pale green dress. Underneath, I wore a completely unnecessary bra with clear plastic straps. I looked at my flat chest in the mirror, grabbing a few pieces of toilet paper to shove in my bra. Inhaling deeply, I tried to puff up my chest to give any semblance of boobs. Nothing.

When I arrived at the church reception hall, only a handful of older guests were there, presumably Valerie's relatives.

Two ushers were helping a Baker position Valerie's cake on the center table while her Aunt Luisa supervised, even with only a month of Spanish under my belt, I could tell she was giving orders to ensure the cake was perfectly angled for photos. From the distance I was standing, I could only make out the very top cake tier. A cursive "15" cake topper.

Valerie's damas came in all together–everyone except Mariah. No doubt the whole family got ready in the morning. They all looked beautiful and womanly in their pale green dresses. Sally looked like she could have passed for a college student. I tugged at the waist of my dress. Maybe it was good that I hadn't seen the cake. If I had a single bite, I'd have a food-baby for the rest of the night, making my complete lack of figure look even more like a toddler's.

The hall filled more and more with guests when finally the guest of honor arrived. Valerie was radiant. She looked like the beautiful porcelain doll had come to life. Every strand of hair was perfectly in place, ringlet curls cascading out of her tiara. The dusty pink version of the doll's darker gown made Valerie's brown skin glow.

The time came for the rest of the court to leave. We were going in the back room to prepare for the grand entrance. The familiar 8-count waltz music came on. I took Carlos's hand high in the air and followed the other couples out.

This time, Sr. Molina was not counting out loud for us, but my partner was muttering under his breath.

"Forward, Step, Sweep, Together," Carlos whispered.

I giggled just loud enough for him to hear. He looked up at me instead of his feet and grinned. Through his smile, I could still make out his lips "Backward, Step, Sweep, Together."

Between all of the practices at the Molinas (and my own secret practices in my bedroom at home), I had gained enough confidence for the steps themselves. I whispered the steps back to Carlos. Together, we chanted our way through the familiar song.

This was the first time in all these weeks that I actually noticed Carlos's hand. This was a waltz, so our positioning dictated that his hand would be at the small of my back. It was at a respectful height, of course. I wondered if I had a crush on him. I didn't see how. I'd barely spoken to him, really, mostly just hung out with the girls, but as we danced in our fancy clothing, I wondered if I was *supposed* to have a crush on him. He certainly *smelled* better at this dance than at any of our practices.

We danced through to our next marked position in the hall. Here, it was the punch area—at the Molina's it was the blue chair that Sr. Molina marked for us. I felt the pain in my stomach again. The one I'd been feeling for weeks, but this time it was bigger. Any chance of having a crush on Carlos had ended. I needed to go to the bathroom after this song was over.

Glide, Step, Sweep, Together, Twirl, Around, and Dip.

That was it, that was the end. The guests applauded, the music instantly got more modern, and I discreetly made my way to the bathroom.

Safely in the stall, I inspected my underwear.

Nothing?!

STILL. Not a drop of blood. I had read *every* article online about periods. I knew that girls tended to get synced up and I was hanging out with these girls non-stop; I knew the cramping feeling was on the lower abdomen (exactly where my stomach was hurting); I knew it messed with emotions, and I was feeling awful. Every bit of foreshadowing was pointing to finally starting my period at Valerie's Quinceañera. But there was nothing. I was a high schooler with no period. A Toddler. What else could I possibly do? My eyes started to water as I stared at the dry pantyliner that I'd prepped.

I heard the outer door open, and I flushed immediately. I had to pull myself together fast–God knows the only thing worse than someone coming in and thinking you're *crying* in the stall is someone coming in and thinking you're *pooping* in the stall.

I opened the door to see Valerie, dressed in her beautiful gown. I hadn't had the chance to talk to her all evening-being the guest of honor meant she was far too busy chatting with relatives to actually talk to us.

"You look so beautiful!" I told her, giving her a hug.

"Oh thank you!" she said. To my surprise, she pulled down the upper part of the bodice to reveal a black strapless bra. "Check this out, isn't it ridiculous?" At that moment, I noticed the bodice was lined with such thick padding in the breasts she completely took a different shape.

"I keep thinking back to Sally's Quince last year when I was a dama and my boobs were mosquitos. Now I realize that none of us are like Sally and it's all fake and pretentious."

Valerie hopped into the stall in a hurry–this was her day so there was no time for a lengthy conversation.

I made my way back to the hall just as the cake was being wheeled to the center of the room. I could almost smell the sugary icing breeze past me as the waiters brought it into position. This time, I had to get a good look.

I moved myself toward the other damas and took in the sight of the beautiful cake.

It was a beautiful four-tiered pink cake, slightly paler than the Last Doll's dress, but following the same theme. White royal icing lined the edges, and flakes of gold pulled together any time two designs crossed, giving it a beautiful glowing effect. Valerie had told us earlier that the cake had a different flavor on each tier. From bottom to top, *Vanilla-Raspberry* (a crowd pleaser), *Black Forest Gateau, Almond and Lemon,* and topped off with *Red Velvet.*

The cake topper I'd seen earlier with the number "15" pulled the ensemble together. A beautiful cake to celebrate my beautiful--and equally insecure--new friend.

Valerie hurried gracefully from behind me to meet up with her gorgeous cake. I was reminded of every single princess who holds up her ball gown as she hustles away with the clock nearing midnight. I didn't see how this girl could even have an ounce of insecurity.

I clapped with the crowd as my new friend cut a slice out of the top tier of her cake. Her knife sliced through the sponge just under the glittery "15" that graced the top.

The cut revealed a deep red velvet sponge. Valerie and Mariah carefully placed it on a plate and handed it to a server. The cake was served.

That red velvet sponge was the only red I would be seeing that night, but that was okay. We were all desperately trying to be something else, to grow up faster.

Who knows, Cinderella may have even stuffed her Godmother's dress with a few dish rags.

Step 2

Add Eggs, Flour, Sugar, Butter

Cake Challenge!

I walked into Chemistry with a spring in my step and an eighth of an inch of midriff exposed above my low-rise bell bottoms. Just enough to be trendy, not enough to be dress-coded. I had just heard from Mariah that she heard from Valerie that Ryan Ellis told Carli's brother Brian that I had a "Rockin bod."

Let me reiterate - Ryan Ellis, *ahem* a sophomore *ahem* (and a cute one at that) thought that I had a "Rockin Bod." *ME!*

"What's up?" he said (a linguistic genius.)

I smiled. My knees went weak and I took my seat next to him—alphabetical order assigned seating had played to my favor the entire semester. Unfortunately, at the beginning of the year, Ryan was seeing Lucy Dunphy, But about three weeks before the "Rockin' Bod" comment, I'd heard a rumor that he and Lucy broke up around Valentine's Day. Lucy and I had only met a handful of times, so there would be no Girl Code broken if I pursued Ryan.

"Hi," I replied back, kicking myself internally for not thinking of something witty or cute.

That was it, what else could I possibly say? This was Ryan Ellis. This was Sophomore Chemistry. I was a freshman on foreign soil.

I watched the clock tick behind Mrs. Beauchamp for the next hour and a half, counting down the minutes until study hall and the chance to finish our conversation.

We were going over chemical changes - when molecules that compose two or more substances combine to create a new substance. At the molecular level in chemical change, the atomic bonds will be broken, causing the atoms to rearrange themselves and form something completely new. For example, $2\,H_2O \rightarrow H_3O^+ + OH^-$. Mrs. Beauchamp reached in her drawer to pull out a few pennies for a second example. The class groaned as we'd all completed the penny-to-copper experiment back in sixth grade.

I glanced at the clock again. 11:11. I silently wished to myself that Ryan Ellis also happened to have a crush on me and that he would ask me out. I glanced over at him. He was doodling on his paper as always. I watched the tendons on his right-hand flit about while his sketch took shape. He didn't seem to be drawing anything in particular, just designs to fill the time. I was more focused on his wrists–they were *guy* wrists; wide, even though he was quite skinny. *Mature*, I thought, imagining his hand holding mine.

His sketching slowed, and I drew my attention back to the front of the class, sensing he might notice me looking at him. My face prickled with embarrassment.

Mrs. Beauchamp pipetted vinegar onto several pennies and assured us we'd be looking again at the pennies throughout the week as they turned green. The formula was written out on the board behind her, which we'd be quizzed on later.

Finally, 11:45 rolled around and it was time for study hall. We were free to our own devices.

"Oh, it's Amanda's birthday tomorrow!" I reminded Ryan.

Amanda was a mutual friend from JROTC. A senior, and arguably the only JROTC student to be considered a social butterfly at Hamilton

High School. She was just about the nicest person on the planet and took all of us younger JROTC kids under her wings. She was turning eighteen, so I was going to make her a strawberry cake to commemorate her. I'd never decorated a cake before, but I thought I could cut it out into the shape of an A and give it to her.

"Yeah I know, I'm going to bake her a cake," said Ryan.

I wasn't sure how to handle this news - This was *Ryan Ellis*- the soon-to-be love of my life- but he was going to make a cake for Amanda? *No way.*

"You're going to *what*?" I teased back, "I was 100% planning to make her one too. Back off!"

"Mmm," Ryan paused. I noticed he had stubble coming in under his chin. "I bet mine would be better."

I shifted to my desk. "I seriously doubt that."

"Is that a challenge, Crownover?" Last Name drop.

This is my moment! I thought, *he is definitely flirting.*

"Absolutely it is," I flirted back, hoping it was successful.

"See, but I think you're only saying you're going to make her a cake because I did." he said, "so now I'm a bit skeptical."

The conversation went on until we decided, now, with Amanda facing two cakes to celebrate her birthday, we'd both deliver one and have her judge which one was better.

We outlined the rules of our challenge;

1. Cake must be made at home (not bought from a store)
2. If you use mix, you have to add something other than cake mix. It didn't matter what. Fruit, 7-up, sour cream, etc. Something to make it unique.
3. Amanda will judge which cake is superior in appearance and taste on her birthday.

We shook on our deal, causing sparks to fly further.

"You're going to forget." Ryan asserted, still unconvinced that I had truly planned to make Amanda a birthday cake.

"I am not, I already bought the ingredients" – a lie, but I'm sure my parents had something in the cabinet. "How do we know you won't forget?"

Ryan took out his sharpie and wrote CAKE in large chicken scratch across his forearm.

"Here," Ryan said, gesturing for permission to grab mine.

I offered my arm out and he took my wrist in his hands. I bit my lip and watched as he outlined the word "Cake" on my forearm in almost graffiti-style bubble letters. His hands were steady. The pressure from the Sharpie tip driving along my skin made me want to inch closer to him. Ever the artist, he added two more colors to outline his initial word.

"There," he said. "Now neither of us will forget."

The bell rang on a perfect cue.

"Cake challenge!" He said with a wink, gesturing to his chicken-scratch tattoo.

"Cake challenge!" I repeated back. I took a deep breath to settle the butterflies, running my fingers gently along my new Sharpie tattoo.

* * *

That night, I raided my parents' cabinets for any sort of boxed cake mix and topping. I settled on a strawberry flavor from *Betty Crocker* and followed the directions to a T. It was, technically speaking, the first time I'd ever made a cake by myself.

The oven was set to 350 degrees and inside a chemical change was happening. The molecules of the baking soda and egg all swirled together as the heat from the oven left the cake to rise. Chemistry.

When the cake was ready, I carved the pieces, rearranging some of the sponge to form an "A" for Amanda on the serving platter. I was here to impress an artist like Ryan Ellis. This needed to look the part.

After carving, I stepped back to admire my work. The base "A" was solid. With smooth clean lines, it looked just like a typed Arial letter. I taste-tested some of the scrap sponges that didn't make it into the piece. Crumbly strawberry sponge melted in my mouth. I was sure this was going to be great.

I slathered on some icing as neatly as I possibly could, learning only afterward that you have to wait for the cake to cool *completely* before putting your icing on.

Pink icing dripped down the edges, revealing the pink-stained sponge on the surface of my cake letter. Betty Crocker had helped me make a perfectly adequate–if a bit runny– A-shaped cake to give to Amanda. At least it tasted okay.

* * *

Ryan Ellis never followed through with his side of the Cake Challenge, but in college five years later, he *did* ask me to send him nudes. I wonder if he still has them...

Getting Baked at Sweet Sixteen

"Bye Mom, see ya tomorrow!" I hugged Mom a quick goodbye before hopping out of her Subaru.

Mariah greeted me in the front yard, as planned. "Hey birthday girl! I'm so excited for our sleepover!"

Mom and Mariah exchanged greetings, and we lingered in the front yard, expecting Mom to drive off. It was dark out–she was clearly waiting to make sure we got inside safely. The only problem–Mariah's family was not expecting me for a sleepover. This was just cover for us to get to the party at Brian's house.

"Here–let's go in through the side gate," Mariah whispered. She followed with a loud "Bye Mrs. Crownover" directed at my mom.

Mom stayed in her car as Mariah and I made our way past the wooden gate to the backyard. When we got to the other side and latched the gate, we knelt down, staying absolutely still so our shadows wouldn't move. I watched through a knot in the wood as Mom drove off.

Success.

"Okay cool, I have to get back inside before *my* mom wonders where I am," said Mariah. The dogs are inside, so you're good to stay here until Evan and Valerie pick you up."

"You'll come by later?" I asked.

"Of course! Alex goes to bed at 7, then mom pretty much locks herself in with *Greg* for the rest of the night." Mariah stuck a finger down her throat to mimic gagging at the thought of her mom and stepdad having sex in the room next to hers. The couple had gotten married the year before and were on each other like... well *worse* than teenagers. Valerie and Evan's libidos couldn't even hold a candle to Mariah's mom. Still, newlywed parents were a good cover for sneaking out. And this was a night to sneak out.

Big Adam and I shared a birthday two years apart, and with Zach Cross's parents out of town for the weekend, our mutual friend kindly offered to host our combination sweet sixteen and milestone 18th birthday. The guys were already there (they didn't have curfews to worry about). It took a bit more coordination and planning to get the girls to Zach's house.

"Is it okay if I call you when I get there?" I asked "I'm almost out of texts."

"Ugh, you need a better phone plan." Mariah breathed a dramatic sigh.

"Well, *I'm* sorry, not all of our parents marry real estate moguls who can afford unlimited minutes." I teased.

"Oh, how *tragic*," Mariah feigned a swoon. "My parents actually love each other, so they don't compete for their children's affection by buying them things."

I rolled my eyes at her jeers, but she was right. I really didn't have anything to complain about, but my functional middle-class two-parent household was frankly boring compared to the stories my friends came to school with.

"But really I gotta get inside." Mariah added, opening the door to the laundry room at the side of her enormous house "I want you shitfaced by the time I arrive!"

With that, Mariah held up a finger like a Sunday school teacher as she closed the side door to her house.

It wasn't long before Evan's 1996 Pontiac pulled up about a block away from Mariah's McMansion. The car flashed its headlights three times, so I knew it was them.

Valerie, Evan, and I arrived at Zach's tiny one-story house in the neighborhood just north of Loop 101. As I'd assumed, the guys were already there, and drinking out of stereotypical red solo cups. I widened my eyes at the size of the party. There had to be at least 30 people inside– way larger than anything I'd ever been to. If Zach lived in Mariah's neighborhood, it would have looked like it was straight out of a teen movie.

"Heyyyyy!" the crowd generally shouted together as Valerie and I took off our shoes. A scrawny guy I didn't recognize was still upside down over the keg.

"BIIIIIRTHDAAAAAY GIIIIRRRRRRRL" Big Adam's voice boomed from his lawn chair in the living room.

If you were to ask anyone at Hamilton High School if Big Adam and I were friends, hell, if Big Adam and I even knew each other, they would unanimously say, "Not a chance." I was a junior. An awkward, quiet, JROTC Cadet Lieutenant in AP classes. Big Adam held celebrity status among the Seniors. For one, you can't miss him. At 6'2" and 350+ pounds, Big Adam could be found from any angle in Hamilton High School's hallway, cracking some kind of joke that would reverberate his voice across the whole campus. But our birthdays drew us together each fall for the celebration.

Let's be real, this was always Adam's party, but I wasn't about to turn down free alcohol.

"Birthday Boy!" I yelled back shakily. Even if I had been as drunk as those guys, I wasn't one to be loud.

"As I remember, you're a Kahlua fan?" Ryan Ellis's voice snuck up on me from behind.

I turned and my freshman-year crush offered me a shot glass. He was referencing the previous Adam Birthday Party in which I, never having tried alcohol, got completely wasted on *Kahlua*.

"Har har" I mocked back, grabbing the shot.

He poured one for himself. Ryan had grown a fauxhawk, something that would become his signature style for the next three years. He looked different than he did back in Chemistry Freshman Year. It was now dyed green and a bit wild for me, but I still had a soft spot for him. "Happy birthday!" He added, tilting the drink toward me in cheers.

I smiled and took a sip of the sticky liquid coffee. The truth was, Kahlua wasn't just my favorite alcohol I'd tasted, it was the *only* one. I was by no means a partier, and Big Adam's 17th Birthday last year was the first and last party I'd been to.

I thanked Ryan for the drink.

Nervous that Big Adam didn't hear my initial birthday wishes, and honestly unsure of what else to say to Ryan, I decided to make my way across the cramped living room.

"Sixteen, right?" Big Adam bellowed, seeing me approach.

"Yep! Eighteen?"

"EIGHTEEEEEEN!" he shouted, raising his PBR can to the crowd from his seat.

"EIGHTEEEEEN!" several guys echoed back.

"We need more ladies here!" Big Adam complained. "When are the *women* getting here?" (What was I? A lampshade?)

As if it was planned, the front door burst open. Mariah and Sally walked in. Mariah was carrying a grocery store cake with "Happy Birthday Rhonwyn" piped onto the top.

"WHERE'S MY BIRTHDAY GIRL?" screamed Mariah.

Mariah's thick, loving arms wrapped around me in an embrace. I was glad she could make it. I hugged her back, despite seeing her only two hours earlier. It was high school, and as everyone knows, high school friendships are felt with such passion that you have to hug each time you see each other. It was as though every sighting of a friend may be the last time. Maybe that's the better mindset.

"Ugh, these aren't women, these are *girls*" mocked Big Adam, who only saw us as his kid brother's age. (Fun fact; Adam's brother Kyle was actually *bigger* than Big Adam in both height and weight, but Adam's moniker was set before Kyle hit puberty, so "Big Kyle" never became a thing.)

The girls brought the cake to the table alongside the plastic shopping bag. They immediately began pulling the other materials from the bag. The candles, I recognized. The lighter made sense. You know, to light the candles. The sheets of paper seemed... odd. That is until Sally took out a bag from her pocket and started pouring it onto one of the sheets.

"It's *salvia*" she explained, "apparently you hallucinate, and it doesn't show up on a drug test."

Mariah lit the candles on my cake–a cake with only my name on it. I looked at the plastic lid, which read "Dr. Pepper Cake" with Dr. Pepper's Logo front and center – It looked like a standard chocolate cake, but I was willing to try *anything* that night.

Apparently, Dr. Pepper adds sweetness and moisture to the chocolate, giving it a unique melt-in-your-mouth flavor while remaining light and fluffy.

The party, which had somehow grown even *more* crowded by the time the candles were lit, started singing happy birthday. I felt loved and surrounded by friends until they got to the "Happy Birthday dear *Big Adam*" part. That's when I remembered I was a nerd, and this was Adam's party. Only a handful of guests even knew I existed, let alone that I shared a birthday with Big Adam himself.

When the singing was over, I found a corner to enjoy my cake. I nursed another shot of Kalua in an oversized solo cup and took bites of the equally sweet Dr. Pepper Cake, not a care in the world about how much sugar I was consuming.

Evan approached me with a rolled joint. Evan and I had become good friends since he'd been seeing Valerie. I was relieved to see him. "No pressure," he said, "but thought I'd share."

I had said it about the Dr. Pepper cake. I was willing to try *anything* that night. I nodded and took the joint. He explained to breathe it in and hold it for a few seconds before exhaling. I followed the directions. He took another hit but didn't offer it back.

"*You* should probably stop at the one." He advised, adding shortly after "WHAT ABOUT A SNOWMOBILE!"

With that, he was off, and my eardrum rang for a few seconds from his shouts.

The party had already dwindled as the guys chased Evan around while he searched for his "snowmobile." Valerie and Mariah joined each other on the couch, not wanting to get involved in the guys' antics. More and more people left the party as curfews were hit and things got a bit too weird. I settled in. I had an alibi since my parents thought I was at Mariah's house, and I knew that Mariah would be in it for the long term. I was sixteen. I had no idea where I was going to be the next morning, but it didn't matter.

Quite suddenly, time seemed to slow down and speed up all at once.

I was transfixed by the heat of my breath at the back of my throat. It was warmer than normal, *like steam*. I thought. I wondered why my throat would know the difference between steam from my breath versus water. *There are particles of water in the steam, and yet my throat knows to breathe in and out.*

I was definitely high.

I bit into my Dr. Pepper cake. It was *truly* divine. I thought about the idea of a Dr. Pepper Carrot cake–Dr. Pepper himself, but instead of a nose, he'd have a carrot. Like a snowman? I laughed to myself. Is that who was driving Zach's snowmobile?

Evan and Valerie left. Presumably, this was to make out in Evan's car and drive Valerie home.

Mariah, Big Adam, Zach, and myself were left in the quiet after-party. Red solo cups and empty beer cans were littered across the tiny living room.

Too exhausted to do anything about the mess, the four of us settled in under blankets and opened the windows. Zach wanted to at least rid the house of the smell of alcohol and smoke. We turned on Finding Nemo as a background movie, and our eyes drew heavy.

"I'm going to text my dad," Big Adam's arm was wrapped around me, which I realized must have happened at some point during Finding Nemo. I didn't mind. I didn't *like-him-like-him,* but I also didn't mind. He was warm and comfortable. He pulled out his *Razor* Phone to text, and the bright blue screen light pierced my eyes. "How does this look?"

DAD

Hey sleeping @ Zach's 2nite. No drugs/drinks.

The decently-sized slice of cake I'd eaten earlier had a sobering effect on me. Know-it-all Rhonwyn was returning, and she was bringing some *edits* with her. "Maybe don't write the part about the drugs and the drinking? Because if you *weren't* doing those things, you wouldn't have brought it up?"

"You're riiiight," Big Adam sounded enlightened as he backspaced his text. He paused and looked me in the eyes. "You're *indispensable,*" he added in a hushed voice.

"You're *drunk.*" I slurred back, barely able to keep my eyes open "Is the alarm set for 7?"

"Yeah" sighed Zach, who by that point was curled up with Mariah somewhere behind us on the bed.

"Good." I said, drifting off to the sounds of Dory's "Just Keep Swimming."

* * *

The next morning, I startled awake to Zach's bedroom door swinging wide open. A silhouette of a little boy stood in the doorway, backlit by the bright morning sunshine.

Adam, Mariah, Zach, and I were all curled up on the bed together. I vaguely remembered that Mariah and I took our jeans off at some point in the night after the rest of the party left. We determined it was more comfortable to sleep in only our underwear. I was horrified. Nothing had happened (aside from drinking and smoking), but this looked *really bad*.

"Hector, what are you doing in here!?" Zach jolted out of bed.

Mariah pulled the covers over her chest--apparently, she had taken even more clothes off throughout the night.

"Get out of my room!" Zach screamed, throwing a pillow at his brother.

The pitter-patter of Hector's footsteps faded into the distance as he ran across the house.

I flipped my phone open to check the time. My screen had broken three days prior. A black blob covered the whole left quadrant of the screen, and the rest was showing nothing but pixelated lines. I could vaguely make out 9:45AM in the corner.

Oh no, I thought.
Oh no oh no oh no.

The pitter-patter returned, drawing nearer. This time, it was accompanied by a steadier, heavier cadence. Zach's mom.

Dressed only in a bra and underwear, (though, who was I to judge, based on my outfit) Mrs. Cross slammed the door open to Zach's room, screaming something in Spanish that I didn't understand. *I really needed to get better at Spanish.*

All four of us jumped to our feet to get our clothes back on. Mariah was nearly in tears. I tunnel-visioned myself to only focus on getting my pants zipped.

We joined Big Adam, Zach, and Mrs. Cross in the kitchen. She was finishing up a phone call with Big Adam's dad. "You come get him. I am not happy this is the second time I caught your son with mine, both smelling like alcohol! Second time! Talk soon."

Big Adam's giant personality from last night was minuscule next to the fury of Mrs. Cross. He sat slumped in his chair, awaiting his fate.

Mrs. Cross slammed the landline back into the receiver and directed her gaze to Mariah and me. We're next.

"I need to call your parents *now*," demanded Mrs. Cross, pulling the wall phone back from the receiver, just as enthusiastically as she'd slammed it down. "Give me their numbers."

Mariah was fully sobbing by this point, breathing heaves between tears, so Mrs. Cross looked at me to go first. *Damn my lack of outward emotional response.* Not having my own mother's phone number memorized, I flipped my phone open to read it to her.

Fuck. I remembered. *My screen's broken.*

"I ..." My heart was racing from my own stupidity making an already horrible situation worse. We were caught and now *I'm an absolute idiot.* I started to explain, "...I don't know my mom's number, and my screen is broken, so I can't even–"

"Don't lie to me little girl, you give me your mother's number. You come into my house, sleep under my roof, drink my alcohol without my knowledge and you tell me you don't know your own mother's number." She moved on to Mariah, who was just catching her breath.

"What about you? Sleeping in my son's bed. He is seventeen years old, I am not going to become a grandmother today."

Mariah dialed a number in her own phone and put it on speaker. It rang and rang, but there was no answer.

"My parents are out of town," Mariah lied, "I don't think they'll pick up. If I can go home with Rhonwyn–"

"I don't care where you go, I need you both out of my house, away from my boys, but I'm not letting you out without giving you to a parent."

"Mrs. Cross" I pleaded softly, showing her my damaged phone, "I promise I'm not lying, I just don't have my mom's number memorized. Can Mariah call our friend Valerie? She'll have it, and then we can call my mom."

Reluctantly, Zach's mom agreed, leaving to put her own on clothes while we played telephone to search for my own mom's number.

Once we procured the number from Valerie (who wished us the best of luck in our upcoming groundings) Mariah looked at me desperately "Can I just go to your house? My mom's gonna lose her shit if he finds out. Your parents are normal."

"Sure" I agreed.

It was true that my parents were normal. Growing up, they never raised their voices to me or each other. If they were disappointed in someone in the family, they'd just gossip about them at the dinner table. I followed the rules to not disappoint them, but this was a big disappointment, and I had no idea what to expect.

Mrs. Cross returned, dressed in a bright purple t-shirt. She dialed my mom's number.

"Hello?" I heard the faint sound of my mom's voice from the phone. I winced at the conversation I was about to put her through.

"Hello, Mrs. Crownover? Do you know where your daughter is right now?"

"Um" my mom paused, she's an introvert like I am. This kind of on-the-spot trick question is not her forte. "She is supposed to be at a friend's house."

"Oh, she's not at a *'friend*'s house.'" Mrs. Stone mocked, "She is at MY HOUSE. I found *your* daughter naked in my son's bed this morning, smelling like alcohol and weed."

Okay, I thought, *technically not naked, technically not weed, and technically not in the bed either. I was near Big Adam, not by Zach in the bed. My mom deals with facts, let's stick to facts.* I dared not say anything to Mrs. Cross.

"Oh... oh my god, I can't believe that." I heard my mom from the other end "I'll come to get pick her up. What is your address?"

When the conversation was through, Mariah, Adam, and I sat in silence on the living room couch while Mrs. Cross screamed at Zach in the kitchen. I nervously fiddled with my thumb ring. My parents had just gotten it for me a few days before for my sweet sixteen. Rainbow cubic zirconia circled the ring. It was cute. For their sixteen-year-old who just disappointed them. My stomach churned from the combination of worry and alcohol.

Suddenly,

POW!

The incomprehensible chastising from Mrs. Cross was interrupted by a loud skin-to-skin contact sound that reverberated through the kitchen and living room.

Startled, I turned around to look through the archway into the kitchen. Zach was clutching his jaw. Mrs. Cross was clutching his hair with her left hand as she took another swing. This time it was closed-fisted at Zach's cheek. Zach was no Big Adam. Yet, it was a sight to see my muscular friend get taken down by his own mother who came only about up to his shoulder in height.

Zach sat down in a kitchen chair, defeated, leaving his mother with the added height comparison. The conversation was over.

Mrs. Cross turned to walk away and her eyes met with mine. "What are you looking at girl?"

"Nothing, ma'am," I said, knowing when to use my JROTC responses.

* * *

My parents probably Googled "How to ground your daughter" that night. What they came up with... I had to turn my (broken) phone in every evening at 8 PM. This wasn't nearly as big of a deal in 2007 as it would be to a teenager today. I also had to make a spreadsheet providing my parents with a list of all of my friends' names in column A and their parents' names & phone numbers in column B.

That was it. That was the grounding.

"Your parents are normal" – Mariah's statement echoed in my head as I entered the numbers into my spreadsheet. She never told her parents that she got caught. I didn't know her enough yet to know whether her parents would react like Zach's mom or worse, but that statement stuck with me.

Watching Zach's mom slug him with all her might that morning, despite the obvious stature disparity, I could tell it wasn't the first time. I imagined him at his little brother Hector's age clutching his face after he did something wrong. I envisioned a 10-year-old Zach getting hit for breaking a vase while wrestling inside, or stealing from the cookie jar.

My parents are normal. I was lucky. But somehow that made me feel even worse. "We aren't mad," they told me, "just disappointed."

My first love was Pi

I can't write a memoir about cake without mentioning my first love, pi. Pi always follows the same recipe; whether you're 13 or 30. That first treat. Something new. Pi gets your heart racing with just one whiff. With Pi, you experience that hot rush of blood pumping through your veins when you bring the sweet, silky filling to your lips...

I'm getting ahead of myself, aren't I?

They say you never forget your first love. My first love, my first *real* love, was in 11th grade; and our story started with pi. Pie served a la mode at Village Inn of course. It was March 14th, 2008. Pi Day; 3.14. Get it? *Pi Day.*

The butterflies had been there for a couple of weeks, but we'd known each other much longer. Dustin Srinivas was a huge nerd, just like me. He was studious, ranking in the top 15 of the student body, but he was far from being an outcast. Always the class clown–or at least, as much of a class clown as you can be in AP US History–I knew Dustin to be in the background, cracking jokes in nearly every circle of friends I found myself with. Dustin was great friends with Carlos, who I danced with at Valerie's Quinceañera. He was at my (read: *Big Owen's*) birthday party the year before. Somehow, Dustin was a friend of a friend of *everyone* I knew, but we didn't notice each other until the start of Junior year.

We got to know each other sitting together in 11th-grade English. That's about as much of a social life as I could muster early that semester. I was still serving a months-long grounding sentence from Zach's party. It took about 6 months of chatting in First Hour English before Dustin worked up the courage to ask me out. Pi Day was our first official date.

Believe it or not, Village Inn hadn't started capitalizing on Pi Day in 2008. We were true nerds, arriving at Village Inn to order Pie on Pi Day, and it was our own idea.

The restaurant was about as cookie-cutter as you'd expect. Framed photos of breakfast food lined the walls. Inside, waiters and waitresses who I went to school with served food to the elderly. We were the youngest customers by about half a century. I wondered if that would be us one day–if we'd be the high school sweethearts that made it through the years. It was silly to wonder on a first date, but I can't say it didn't cross my mind. In the fluorescence of the restaurant, I felt over-exposed and self-conscious. I knew he liked me, but now he could *see* me. Face to face, instead of next to each other in class. The only comfort was I could also see *him*.

My heart fluttered as I looked at the boy I was on a date with. Mariah's Akita had taken a bite out of his right eyebrow the month before, and he still had two stitches covering the fresh scar. He styled his dark brown hair in the shaggy 2008 style toward his stitches to cover them up.

"Does it still hurt?" I asked him, looking at the scar.

Self-consciously, Dustin reached a hand up to his eyebrow. "Not really. it just feels really dry when I move my eyebrows." He added to the effect by making his eyebrows do the worm across his forehead, stopping in goofy Zoolander or Dr. Evil expressions.

I was still giggling by the time the waitress arrived. I ordered my favorite - their Caramel Pecan Silk Pie. The waitress compared it to a

French silk pie with chocolate mousse filling, tons of whipped cream, and a flaky crust. What made Village Inn's so unique was the Caramel layer for an added sweetness and pecans for crunch.

Dustin ordered the Chocolate Peanut Butter Cup with ice cream. All sugar. A classic. I love Reese's as much as the next girl.

Our spoons clinked as we tasted each others' pies, a small act, but sharing food was something I only ever did with close friends or family. Another jolt surged through me as our spoons touched, but this one wasn't electric. It was sure, steady, and comfortable. We could have been just like the old couple next to us sharing our pies and seeing which one tasted better.

Dustin flipped open his phone and rolled his eyes.

"Ugh, my mom is telling me to steal the menu," he said, snapping the phone shut.

"Steal the menu?" I repeated, intrigued.

I'd met Dustin's mom a few times that year, and I already adored her. Tracy was nothing like my mom. She was loud, she loved to dance, and she was home all day. I was intrigued to reveal another layer of her personality.

"Yeah, she likes to steal menus from restaurants so she can recreate the meals at home," Dustin explained.

"She knows they're all online right?"

"She knows that," he conceded, "but she started collecting so long ago that she wants a whole set."

I played lookout as Dustin snuck the grimy Village Inn menu into his backpack. We giggled the whole way out of the restaurant and out to his 2001 Forerunner. The heist was complete, and we were off to the movie.

I paid for the tickets at the counter. The feminists that we were, we'd established early in the planning that we'd "go Dutch." Dustin would buy the pie, but I'd get the movie tickets. Of course, we had the metabolism of teenagers, so we also ordered popcorn.

I have no memory of what movie we were watching. Seriously. I Googled it for this chapter, and there's nothing good in the spring of 2008, but surely we watched *something*.

We couldn't have been far into the movie by the time the popcorn was finished. Dustin folded up the bag and put it under his cup, then returned his right arm to our side-by-side armrests. The movie was still playing, but the sound was muffled by the ringing bells in my head. Dustin's hand was inches from mine. Time turned into slow motion.

Exhale.

I could feel his arm gently graze against my own—not enough to touch skin, but enough to feel he was there. My left pinky started to draw closer to his, willing him to make the first move.

Inhale.

I bit my bottom lip absentmindedly. I was nervous. I wanted to fidget my toes, pick at my cuticles, anything to calm the anxiety, but with my arm next to Dustin's, I held absolutely still.

Exhale.

We were as still as could be, but it seemed our arms were drawing millimeters closer with each passing breath.

Inhale.

Swiftly, confidently, he took my hand.

Time stood still as I exhaled again, intertwining my fingers through his. For the first time in weeks, the butterflies stopped. They were settled, replaced by a jolt of electricity through my whole body.

I'm sure it was a great movie. (Whatever it was.) My sole focus was on Dustin's hand on mine.

* * *

Dustin and I made it through both proms, one terrible job at *Blimpie's*, and a semester of college. He was my first love. My first "I love you," My first time having sex, my first comfortable-enough-to-fart. He was mine and I was his. We thought we'd last forever. We named our hypothetical children and planned to get married on March 14, 2015, signing the certificate at exactly 1:59 PM (not just Pi Day, but Pi *Date*). That of course, never happened.

Dustin also ended up being my first long-distance relationship, my first lover's quarrel, my first break-up, and my first heartbreak. The whole experience, the whole pi(e)--beginning to end.

My first love didn't end up being the love of my life. I wasn't ready for a serious relationship–I had much more growing up to do–but Dustin was funny, and kind, and safe. The type of relationship I would wish for any teenager. He taught me what I should expect from a partner, and what I should expect from myself.

I can't for the life of me remember that first movie we saw together, but I will never forget my first love. Or the first 78 digits of pi.

LOST in Cupcakes

Black Eyed Peas blared from dorm room 317. I could barely hear my keys jingling as I inserted my key into the lock. I covered my ears to the deafening volue of the music, pushing the door open with my shoulder.

"*SERIOUSLY?*" I shouted at my roommate. I tossed my backpack haphazardly onto my bed.

Mariah was curling her hair on *my* side mirror as usual. She turned toward me, keeping her hair steady in the curler, and swinging her hips to the beat.

She replied, "*Them chickens jockin' my style; They try to copy my swagger; I'm on that next shit now*" Or at least...that's what it sounded like she said? Her lips didn't match the music.

I walked across the room to turn the volume down. This was far too jarring right after the deafening afternoon silence that was CHEM 102.

Mariah repeated herself, "I said hey girl! What are you doing here?" She was clearer this time without the music.

"Uh," I gestured to my bed, which Mariah had commandeered via several makeup bags, "I live here too. In case you didn't actually know. That's what I'm doing here."

Mariah raised her eyebrows. "Okay, PMS – Don't worry girl, It's okay the whole floor has it." A tiny bobby pin wobbled between her teeth as she spoke, causing her to lisp her Ts. At that point, she was gathering her hair into a high bun that she'd eventually secure with several of those pins. "No – I mean it's Thursday. Don't you usually hang out with your nerds on Thursdays?"

"What's wrong with my nerds?" I protested.

Mariah and I were best friends in high school, but by the end of our first week at NAU, Mariah had discovered the party scene and I discovered... *Magic the Gathering*. I became fast friends with the nerds of The First Floor in our honors dorm. On Thursdays we watched LOST.

All that came to an end during first-semester finals because of a drunken night with a particularly cute nerd named Mason.

I continued my defense, "Anyway, you know I'm not going to Thursday dinners anymore."

"Because you hooked up with Mason. Are you guys still not over that?" Mariah showered herself in hair spray to complete her signature messy bun style–lest it became neat? I never understood it.

"*Mason and I* are over it. It's his roommate who isn't. So he's starting all these rumors" I took off my jeans and grabbed my crossword puzzle PJs that Mariah had gotten me for my 18th birthday that fall. It wasn't even 5PM, but I'd committed to nights in every single weekday following the night Mason and I hooked up.

"I seriously can't handle how dramatic the love triangle is in your nerd group. It's like a love Tetrahedron. And somehow you and Mason weren't connected in the Tetrahedron, which is why your hookup was SO INSANE. It destroyed...it just destroyed so much."

"Ugh, so I hooked up with Mason, whatever. I'm just tired of the bullying."

"Uh-huh."

"No more Thursday Dinners for me."

"Uh-huh."

"I'm just bummed I'm not going to be able to watch LOST anymore because we don't have a TV. I'm just going to bake some cupcakes."

"Uh-huh."

Mariah unplugged her curling iron. She took a moment to pause before whipping her side bangs as she turned around for dramatic effect. It was a common move of hers.

She began, "One - Stop baking so many cupcakes." Her heavily lined eyes moved up and down as if to judge me from top to bottom. "Not all of us have your metabolism.

'Two. Bull-Fucking-Shit you like LOST. You stopped watching LOST in 10th grade after season 3 like the rest of humanity. Only when *Wes* invited you to LOST were you suddenly like 'Oh it's such a good show, yeah I'll join Thursday dinners.' That's why it was so fascinating to me when you hooked up with Mason, when it was Wes you were pining for all this time. It was the twist I needed though. Fascinating. Can't say you're predictable--"

"I resent that." I held up a finger like a domineering teacher, "If you must know, I don't like Wes. And I do like LOST. And I'm going to watch LOST by myself tonight. I mean, if I'm fortunate enough to get some peace and quiet around here."

"Uh huh... I bet you don't even watch 10 minutes when you're by yourself."

"Challenge accepted." – I crossed my arms.

"Alright, nerd. I gotta go. Sleep with Wes or Mason again or whatever, but keep your Tetrahedron off my bed. No orgies." Mariah grabbed her coat from her Edward Cullen closet.

"Oh my God, Mariah, drop it... I already told you I *do* like Wes. And I *don't like– Wait, shit.*"

"HA!" Mariah pointed a finger at me to celebrate my flub.

"No I mean I don't like Wes and I do like LOST.."

Mariah covered her ears, "LALALA YOU ALREADY ADMIT-TED IT I'M LEAVING NOW ADIOS!"

While I was still sitting on the bed, Mariah wrapped her arms around me, shoving my head into her now 36DD boobs for the duration of the embrace. I returned the hug. "I love you I hate you I figure eight you."

"I love you I hate you I figure eight you," I repeated our special greeting, my voice muffled by her massive breasts.

After our hug, Mariah was on her way. Just as she was motioning to leave, she caught herself at the door. "Oh, you're good watching Harry, right?" Harry, her little blue Betta Fish had lived a freakishly long life throughout High School and moved in with us at the beginning of Freshman year.

"Yeah, we're good." I confirmed, smirking at a second chance at redemption "Harry *loves* LOST."

"And you love Wes, BYEEEE" she screamed dramatically as she left the door.

I hopped off the bed to follow her, "Hey text me when you're home so I know you're safe."

"Don't be a slut!" she called from the hallway.

"Speak for yourself," I muttered to the empty hallway.

I switched off Mariah's stereo completely and adjusted the lights from the fluorescent overhead to our Christmas Light setup. It was just me and Harry the fish. We'd be watching LOST and baking Valentine's Day cupcakes all by ourselves for the evening. The single girl's dream.

Blinding laptop light seared my eyes as I navigated a sketchy website to download the episode. The internet was taking forever. A pixelated porn ad started to play on the right side of the screen. Finally, the main box panned to Evangeline Lily's face. I clicked to expand LOST and cover up the porn.

This was a flash-sideways start to the episode. The fact that flash-sideways even existed was a bit much for me, but I always liked her character.

"I do like LOST," I muttered to Harry, who was circling his bowl.

I settled the laptop on the corner of my desk while I pulled out my mixing bowls and plastic Walmart bag. This single girl had a plan for Valentine's Day Weekend.

I'd prepped for the evening earlier in the week for my chocolate cake bake. I even went as far as giving Mariah's boyfriend $30 to buy me a bottle of Guinness for the batter and a small bottle of RumChata for the icing.

Guinness Cupcakes were a fast favorite of mine. I love them even to this day. When you actually add the beer to the batter, it becomes a bit of a science experiment. The foam reacts so fast to the sour cream that gets added in. It's a rich chocolate sponge when all is said and done. The heady beer plus the sour cream creates that bitter dark chocolate flavor. Sickly sweet RumChata Icing is the perfect match to top it off.

I cracked open the RumChata and took a swig. I wouldn't be needing that much for the recipe...

I mixed the dry and wet ingredients separately as Kate Austen (Evangeline Lily's Character) bent over a taxi cab to deliver Claire's baby. I thought to myself how this was nothing like when Claire was pregnant on the island back in season 1. Claire's romance with Charlie was so sweet, and such a break from the rest of the drama. I rolled my eyes and scooped the flour mixture into the wet bowl. The Guinness tried to fizz with each swirl of the batter.

When the batter was ready, I gathered the bowl and the empty cupcake tray to claim next in line for the 3rd-floor oven. When I got there, the kitchen lights were all out. Of course–Valentine's Day weekend. Everyone was staying the night somewhere *other* than Cowden. Feeling lazy, I decided to hang out in the kitchen while it preheated.

I pulled out my phone. No alerts. It was 5:45 so the guys would be starting to wrap up dinner by then. Certainly, Kevin would be sharing plenty of jokes about how I was going to sleep with everyone on the First Floor. *That sure made for great laughs last time.* Absent-mindedly, I started to slide my finger into the cold chocolate batter–It's always so much better before it's baked.

Licking my finger, I tasted the familiar bitter brew, sour cream, and chocolate, but it was AWFUL. It's always bitter, but this was another level. I spat the mixture in the sink. *I forgot the sugar.* "I'm such a fucking idiot," I whispered as I turned the oven back off. I left the mixture on the counter to grab the missing ingredient.

Returning to my dorm, I found the credits rolling on the show. *I must have missed everything after the opening scene.*

I grabbed the sugar off the corner of Mariah's desk. "I like LOST!" I told Harry, who was laying in his bowl on the other side of it. Even he seemed to think I was covering something up with the whole LOST thing.

Wait...
Laying.... In his bowl. He was *laying*.

I stepped toward the glass to inspect the ancient fish. There he was, floating belly-up near the surface. His feathery fins floated around with the ripples in the water.

"No *no no no no...you can't die now. Your mom just left!"*
Harry was dead.
"Fuck."
Immediately, I grabbed my phone from my back pocket, sliding it open to access the keyboard.

Wes

Harry's dead.

I sat down on Mariah's roller chair and waited for a response. Spinning the chair left and right with an anxious foot, I let my mind wander. Would he even see it, or would he be afraid the guys would see my name at the top and tease him?

Finally, after what seemed like 10 minutes, my phone dinged.

Wes

Who?

Harry. Mar is out of town. Her fish just died.

HAHAHAHAHA

Ass. What should I do?

Flush it.

No! OMG. Come here.

No.

Well what if it's sleeping or something?

Is it belly-up?

Yeah…

Then it's dead.

> Can you please just come here?
>
> Please?
>
> ...I'm making cupcakes!

...I accept this bribe.

Anticipating Wes's arrival, I threw a sports bra on under my crossword puzzle pajama set. I wanted to be clear that I was in for the night and not trying too hard, but I also couldn't *not* try that hard. Tricky double negative. I wanted the medium level of trying.

I examined myself in the mirror quickly. My sparkly blue headband had to go. Taking it off set my bangs into a frenzy, and I wrangled them with a bit of water from the bottle on my nightstand. Finally, I understood the point of Mariah's messy bun.

Minutes later, there was a knock at the door. Followed by a callous "BRING OUT YOUR DEAD."

Wes had arrived with a goldfish net and plastic bag in hand. I grimaced at the thought but directed him toward the bowl.

"Can you make sure he's actually dead please?" I requested. *Can't have me become a fish murderer as well as a slut.*

Wes poked Harry with the net, and the fish floated alongside the top of the water. His little blue body looked like an astronaut, away from his shuttle, unable to control his speed in space. Wes poked harder, jostling the poor thing around. There was no reaction.

"Sorry little buddy." Wes scooped the fish from the bowl. The plastic let out a crinkling sound upon impact as Harry's lifeless body hit the bottom of the bag. Not much of a service for a fish I'd known for an awfully long time.

"I'll go flush him. Meet you back here?"

Glancing at my bed, I worried Wes might have been expecting more than cupcakes as his fish undertaking bribe. *He wouldn't, would he?* I thought to myself. Of course, I had just done my hair before he got there. "The cupcakes though. I'll meet you in the kitchen. They're almost done."

I fixed my sugarless batter and put the cupcakes in the oven as Wes flushed poor Harry's body down the toilet on the first-floor bathroom. The girls' floors were higher in the building, so he had a long journey up and down Cowden's stairs. I set the oven timer. *40 minutes should do it.*

Wes returned to the kitchen and we got to talking while we waited for the treats. We talked about all the normal things college kids talk about–sharing secrets we'd already known about each other and talking about the philosophies that had grown on us through our many eighteen years on Earth. We had a digital friendship from the start. In group settings, we'd barely speak, but follow up the conversation with texts every night. It was a rare chance to talk one on one with him.

The automatic lights flickered off at some point in the conversation and we continued on at the table. I told him about Dustin and how heartbroken I was when we broke up. He told me about the love he still had for his high school sweetheart. We joked about my hookup with Mason. Our conversations went deep but I never felt a spark. It was like I was talking to Mariah, only without the same big personality.

"Are the guys gonna give you a hard time for hanging out with the slut?" I finally asked, knowing that he'd left the Thursday LOST afterparty before it usually concludes.

"You're not a slut. You slept with what, two guys in your whole life? Imagine if we said that about some of the guys on the first floor. Kevin just had his heart broken because he had a crush on you. But it's not right that he said that to you."

"I'm a little bummed you didn't say that on the spot," I told Wes. The shaming had been taking a toll and I wanted someone to speak up for me.

"Yeah, but I'm not a nice guy, and I admit it. Kevin thinks he's a nice guy, but is a dick like the rest of us."

"Mariah says our nerd group is in a love tetrahedron."

Wes let out a chuckle, "Well, even a blind squirrel finds a nut every once in a while."

"Hey," I hit Wes in the arm, half playful, half defensive of my friend, "I do like her most days."

"Eh sorry. You're right. She's just A LOT"

"She is that" I conceded.

The timer in the kitchen echoed louder with each tick. *Did I like Wes?* I wondered.

He was a self-professed "A-hole," but he was always so sure of himself, unlike the other nerds on floor 1. Like me, he liked nerd things, but he also had other interests. He didn't look anything like Dustin or Mason, but he was easy to talk to. It was the week after Valentine's Day. And we were both single...

Wes looked at me. I felt a profound connection to him. He was my friend, maybe even a better friend than Mariah had been the last few months, but there was no spark. I realized this wasn't the type of person I had to put on a fake persona for. Wes never made me feel like I owed him anything in return as so many of the jealous boys in the nerd group had done. He was a friend. An actual friend. With that realization, a massive weight lifted off my shoulders.

Wes broke the silence, "The cupcakes smell pretty g–"

"--I don't think I like you," I interrupted, saying it more for my own sake than his.

Wes looked puzzled. "Gee thanks, well I guess I'll go back downstairs.."

"No, I mean, I don't want to sleep with you or anything." I corrected, meaning to say we were only friends. That comment certainly didn't help get my point across.

"Okay... I didn't ask, but this is not making me feel better, where is this coming from? Do I look fat?"

"No, sorry, I mean, the love Tetrahedron...Mariah said I liked you, and I do, but I don't like you in a romantic... style way." I stumbled through my words as usual when it came to real-life conversations, "And now, Valentine's weekend, we're both single and if anything were going to happen–"

Wes nodded, understanding where I was going with the thought. Even when Wes didn't understand, he always understood. "--it would happen now if it was going to happen. Yeah, I feel the same way." He pulled his glasses off like he always did to think, "Rhonwyn, you're like the girl version of me, which I sometimes need because I'm so stubborn I don't realize when I'm being me. And that's why I always feel like I have to impress you or something, but at the same time, we can never date."

My mind wandered to just a few short hours ago. I thought of myself changing my pajama shirt earlier that night. The messy bun. The worry that he was helping me for a chance at something romantic. I smiled at the absurdity of it all, feeling a sudden wave of clarity. I realized I didn't *have* to have a crush on every guy Mariah teased me about. I didn't *have* to like every TV show my friends liked. I probably could have flushed Harry on my own. What I wanted at that moment was a friend, and I found one.

"You're quickly becoming my best friend, though," I added.

"You're already one of mine," he replied.

"Harry and Hermione?"

"Too soon!" he recoiled, "I just flushed Harry. How about Jin and Sawyer?"

"Yeah, thanks again for that." I laughed, "...can I tell you a secret?"

"Of course, anything."

"I can't *stand* LOST."

The Great Girl Scout Campidemic

"HEY, SHARKTOOTH!?"

"Hey, WHAT?"

"Hey, *KIRSTIN!?*"

"Hey, What?"

"Pass it on!"

The girls at Sharktooth's table gasped at the revelation of their counselor's real name. It had always been Girl Scout Camp tradition to reveal the counselors' names at the final dinner of each session. It was a special treat to close out the week.

"Hey, CAMERA!?" Sharktooth passed along the song to the next counselor.

"Hey, WHAT?!" Camera shouted back.

"Hey, *Kelly!*"

... The name game continued.

I scraped at the icing that topped my modest square of sheet cake. I usually had a small piece every Friday for the festivities. Calories were no concern. I hadn't gotten into the new Fitbit craze, but I would estimate I'd walked about 5 miles a day with those girls. It was back and forth to each activity every week. The walk from Arts and Crafts to the Rock Wall alone was half a mile. I'd more than earned it each week.

Sugar rushed into my mouth as I imbibed in my industrial-style slab of grocery-store cake. Fresh enough, but your basic vanilla buttercream combo. All sugar. No substance. Camp Director Houston (Real name, Jodie) would just buy whatever was on sale and had enough to feed about 85. This week, they'd picked a purple border with blue star sprinkles. She didn't even have them pipe anything on it. There was just cake for the sake of having cake to close out the week.

Frankly, I took the piece of cake just because I did it every week. I'd lost my appetite by Friday Night Dinner since I had spent my entire week cleaning up vomit, after vomit, after vomit.

"THE EPIDEMIC," was what we called it. So many girls came down with some kind of stomach bug that week that we actually had to reorganize the sleeping arrangements to allow the infirmary to expand into the beds at Timber Lodge. The Timber Lodge girls (4th-6th grade) moved in with my 1st-3rd graders in Hedgehog House.

Of course, we had plenty of beds available. The 1st-3rd graders were the first ones to get hit. I only had half my girls left at the table that night. A quarter of them were in the infirmary, the other quarter had been picked up by parents earlier in the week.

I longed to be assigned to Foxtails the next week. I'd even take Timber Lodge--assuming they disinfect it heavily after the girls leave, of course. Being with 5-year-olds while they were sick was pure torture, and I was exhausted from the week we'd endured.

The smell of other people's vomit lingered in the back of my nose.

"Hey, CHIPMUNK!?"
My ears perked at the sound of my camp name. My turn.
"Hey, WHAT!?" I shouted back.
"Hey HANNAH!" I heard my "name" revealed. Oh... did I not mention? Half the time, we counselors made up the "real" names too. Sorry, did I just ruin your childhood?

I never liked my real name revealed because the older girls would always look for us on Facebook after camp ended. With my name, I'm too easy to find.

"Hey, WHAT!?" I leaned my head back to shout my reply.

"Pass it on!"

I looked for another counselor who hadn't been revealed yet.

"Hey PICKLES!?"

"Hey, WHAT!?"

"Hey Taylor!?" – Pickles's name was actually Taylor. I didn't have the energy to think of something creative. They never minded their real name.

"Hey, WHAT!?"

"Pass it on!"

Phew – The best part of the meal is when you know it's not your turn. I slumped in my chair and took another sip of ice water.

"HANNAH-CHIPMUNK!" Payton, one of my 3rd graders pulled at my shirt sleeve. She must have been calling my fake name. "Olivia says her tummy hurts."

I looked at Olivia. She seemed awfully pale. I'd been keeping an eye on her since that morning. She had been looking worse and worse by the hour, surely the next to get hit.

"You okay hon–" I started

"BLEEEEECHHHHH" Olivia let out a demonic croak. Chunky purple cake vomit spewed out of her mouth onto the plate in front of her.

The girls at the table screamed in terror.

Splatters ricocheted onto Charissa and Gretchen who were sitting across the table.

Gretchen started crying.

I sprang from my chair to Olivia, who was still coughing up remnants of icing. *Why would we still give them cake?*

"It's okay." I assured her "Come on, let's get you to Infirmary."

I took in the chaos of the room as I rubbed Olivia's back. Rotor was already on his way to get the kitty litter for the floor. Being unable to tend to the girls in the cabins, the poor male counselors had been relegated to clean-up duty since Wednesday.

* * *

The sun had set by the time I'd left Olivia at Infirmary. The camp would be at Closing Night Bonfire to perform the camper-made skits of the week. I turned right past the rock wall and started making my way toward Song Square where they hosted the campfires. I could see the orange light begin to take in the distance, followed by smoke rising up above the pines. After the week I'd had, I just wanted to lay in the grass and fall asleep under the stars...alone. No more crying girls banging on our cabin door each night. No more cleaning vomit out of sleeping bags.

My stomach churned from the thought of rinsing more puke out of fabric. Or the thought of Olivia at dinner. Or maybe it was just from the cake. Why would *I* have sugar after a day like this?

I inhaled deeply, letting the crisp smell of pine clear my palate. It eased the nausea a bit. *God, I hope I didn't catch this thing*. I thought.

Arriving at Song Square Bonfire, I found a seat in the Hedgehog section right next to my co-counselor, Pickles. The remaining Timber Lodge campers were performing their skit. Two girls were dragging the legs of a third girl across the grass. I wondered if the third girl was supposed to be the wheelbarrow.

"BRING OUT YOUR DEAD!" Yelled the *Wheelbarrow Girl* from the ground.

A fourth camper climbed on top of Wheelbarrow Girl.

The audience roared with laughter. Even Camp Director Jodie let out a chuckle.

Timber Lodge was apparently reenacting their poor counselor Bubbles who'd gotten sick Tuesday. She was so weak that our Lifeguard Rotor used a wheelbarrow from the shed to transport her to Staff House. That's where all the sick counselors were stored.

The skit continued, ending in a chain of Timber Lodge girls being dragged behind the campfire.

"HEAR YE HEAR YE" a final Timber Lodge camper exclaimed, pretending to hold a parchment. "An Epidemic has hit Starry Ranch. Everyone is DEAD." She fell to the ground with a thud of finality.

Timber Lodge got a standing ovation from the audience.

"Thank you, Timber Lodge!" Sharktooth, our emcee of the evening guided the campers off the stage. "Next up we have our youngest campers, but don't let that fool you, they pack a punch–after siesta. Give it up for Hedgehog HOOUUUSE!"

"WOOOOO!" Pickles and I screamed in unison in support of our littles.

Throughout the eight weeks at camp, I'd managed to get assigned Hedgehog House no less than 5 times. Each week I would try to train the girls up in time for Closing Campfire. I wanted the littles to sing just one song that the rest of the camp could decipher.

That week we didn't even prepare a song for them. The Hedgehogs formed a line on the Song Square stage. At once they started to sing two or three different songs. Peyton decided to lie down on the stage, and poor Gretchen's bottom lip was still pouting from the vomit earlier (again, I don't blame her on that one.)

The crowd cheered for our adorable Hedgehogs. Our young campers made their way back to our bench.

Finally, it was time for the counselors to line up and sing TAPS one final time for that week's campers. Out of fourteen counselors, only eight of us were healthy enough to sing. The other six were quarantined down the hill at Staff House.

As the counselors assembled, I heard a cough from Camera.

"No!" Pickles croaked, audibly enough for only the staff to hear. "We can't lose another counselor!"

Camera continued coughing a fit.

I winced, then exchanged a knowing glance with Pickles. *Camera was next.*

Camera ran a few steps away from Closing Campfire, before lurching forward like she'd been kicked in the stomach.

"BLEEEEECHHHHH" Camera's vomit slopped onto the grass. My stomach churned. Adults throwing up was somehow *far* worse than kids.

I closed my eyes tight.

"Let's get her to Staff House." Jodie directed.

"Hey, girls!" Sharktooth was committed to the show, "Don't worry, we're still gonna sing you good night. Hedgehogs, be sure to follow Pickles and Chipmunk after the campfire ends okay? We're gonna take Camera down to the infirmary."

I smiled assuredly at my campers. Pickles and I were down to two for the final evening.

"Fuuuuuuck" Pickles mouthed to me before TAPS began.

I grimaced back at my friend. I couldn't wait to get these campers out of here.

* * *

Pickles and I returned to Hedgehog Staff House after putting the girls down for the evening. The only two left in our staff house of Five.

The radio chirped. "Admin to Hedgehogs. Admin to Hedgehogs."

Pickles grabbed the radio off of Camera's bed. "What's up Admin, It's Pickles."

"So, I know Sharktooth was going to stay with y'all tonight since you're so low staff, but she's feeling sick. She's heading to Staff House now."

Pickles pretended to hit their head on the edge of their bunk. "Yeah," they said unconvincingly "we got it. Campers are asleep now anyway."

"For now" I muttered. We both knew it was only a matter of time before the girls would be knocking on our door again. Homesick, actually sick, have to pee.

'For now." they agreed.

Pickles was out like a light. Lucky.

I dozed in and out, waking up feeling more and more nauseous. Sipping water when I could. I just had to make it through to 10 AM tomorrow. Campers would be gone. We could just sleep and recover until Monday's new arrivals.

I felt dinner and the sugary cake lurching in my stomach. Acid was rising in my esophagus.

Don't throw up. Don't throw up.

Tasting the bile at the base of my throat, I realized I was going to puke before the hour was up. I pulled myself out of bed, careful not to upset my stomach. I extended a foot out to reach my shoes at the base of my bed.

Almost... There... The shoe jiggled a little bit. I couldn't bear to reach down, or I'd puke all over the floor. *Just a bit further...*

Then it came.

I covered my mouth with my hand, but chunks of puke poured out of my mouth and nose. Retching more and more, coughing between each outpour of food and bile.

I gasped and reached for my water bottle. Puke was everywhere.

ChirpChirp.

I heard Pickles' radio turn on. "Hey Rotor," they said flatly into the walkie. "Can you please escort a counselor to Staff House?"

"On my way," a staticky voice in the radio returned.

"It's just me here now" Pickles groaned, "which I will remind you is not actually legal. I'm only one person."

"It's not. I'm on my way with Rotor," Jodie replied on the walkie. "I'll sleep in Hedgehog tonight."

"10-4," confirmed Pickles, dropping the mic on their chest.

Once my puke was cleaned up, I slumped on the porch in front of Hedgehog Staff Cabin, duffel bag in tow. I figured I'd get my plastic drawers after the girls left the next morning. I felt awful. Physically of course, but also terrible for Pickles who was the ONLY counselor left in Hedgehogs. Jodie was there, but we knew she'd be just leading the camp from Hedgehog base.

I heard the Camp golf cart crunching through the gravel path up toward me. It was a step above the wheelbarrow I'd seen Rotor escort Bubbles out of on Tuesday.

As the vehicle slowed to a stop, I noticed that Rotor was wearing a bandana around his nose and mouth like a surgical mask. I wondered if it was even a joke anymore.

"You alright?" Jodie in a low voice so as not to wake the Hedgehogs in the Camper Cabin.

"I just need a shower," I assured her.

She stepped inside the cabin with her overnight bags.

I looked at Rotor who was still behind the wheel of the golf cart.

He tilted his head and with a grave voice whispered "BRING OUT YOUR DEAD!"

Happy Birthday (Cake) to Me!

One late September morning, I curled up in a corner of the Sam's Club breakroom to call The Palace. My birthday was coming up, and I needed to make reservations.

Shortly after Dustin and I broke up a few years prior, I found a little Indian restaurant called The Palace. The Palace reminded me of all the times I was invited to eat out with him and his family, so I soaked my feelings in vindaloo until my heart healed. After that, it was just tradition. 2012 would have been my third birthday at The Palace. The big *21*!

"A reservation for October first?" The man on the phone verified through a thick accent.

"Yes please!" I confirmed, "Eight chairs should do the trick."

"Wonderful, I've got you down for October First."

"Thank you! See you then!"

Soon after, my 15-minute break was over and I had to go back to work. I glanced at the schedule board and groaned - *two clopenings in one week!* And to make matters worse, both of them were on nights I had class. With a heavy sigh, I tied the apron around my waist too tight and headed back to my shift.

The week went by in a blur of clopening, classes, coffee, and repeat. Finally, on the morning of my birthday, I was prepping some muffins when my first customer came in. I breathed a sigh of relief, as the first customer meant my shift was almost over.

The customer was a short Indian man with a flatbed full of food.

"Hi, how can I help you?" I asked, pulling my plastic gloves off as I walked towards the order station.

"Hello! I have a pickup for Vihaan?"

"Sure thing, let me grab that for you."

I walked into the freezer to check for the orders I'd decorated that morning. Pulling out the cookie sheets of orders, I found the one with Vihaan's order slip, remembering his order from the night before. I'd decorated that one. Decorating was a loose term since it was just a frozen cake. One of the other bakers had prepped all the vanilla cakes, so I just had to add "Happy Birthday." No name. Quick and easy.

I brought Vihaan his order, and he thanked me before leaving.

Finally, my shift was over. Friday was my birthday party, and I had the day off. So my to-do list for Thursday was easy. Soak in my bathtub, cuddle up with a book, and my new cat, Virginia, and SLEEP until noon on Friday.

* * *

The usual suspects joined me at The Palace. My best friend, Mariah of course. Daniel, and Abby from Sam's Club, Wes, and Braden. Braden was there with his new boyfriend, Iain. We had to pull up an extra chair since Ian brought his roommate, Derek (more on that later) with him.

Other than Mariah, these were very...how do I put this kindly... *white* friends of mine, so none of them really cared much for spicy food. Or seasoning of any kind. Not to stereotype, but it was pretty true. The spiciest thing I'd known any of them to have in their cabinets was flour. But they showed up for me, hesitantly ordering 1s and 2s on the spice scale.

Iain and Derek were both new to Indian food, so I was excited to share my recommendations and help them order. To my surprise, they both ordered 5s and loved it. I learned that Iain was really into cooking and culture, so he enjoyed trying something new.

As we were finishing up, I was taken by complete surprise when The Palace Owner, Vihaan, came out with a cake filled with candles. I looked at my friends suspiciously, but none of them took the blame for the order.

The waitstaff came out and started to sing as the owner placed the cake in front of me. Behind him was the customer from my shift that week.

"You come here every year," said Vihaan when the singing was over. "We thought we'd say hello and Happy Birthday from us."

I was touched that Vihaan and The Palace had gone out of their way to make this special for me. Vihaan placed the sheet cake in front of me and at the center of the cake –in my own piped handwriting– read, *"Happy Birthday."*

Love at First Cake

"I don't understand what's happening here," I complained to Braden as I ripped into my 14th KitKat wrapper. I broke the KitKat into quads and placed the pieces into the pile with the others.

"They'll wrap all the way around, and it'll kind of look like a fence." Braden's voice was condescending. He gestured in the direction of the cake that he baked the night before. He was always good at that – patience in making the cake one night and decorating the next, that way the icing wouldn't melt on contact. He had way more self-discipline than I could ever imagine, even when it came to baking. *Especially* when it came to baking.

I stared at him blankly as he over-explained the concept of decorating a cake.

He continued. "Then once we have the border, the M&Ms go on top–"

I stopped him before he could go any further, "--No, Jesus. Like, I understand the concept of the cake, the picture's right in front of me."

The cake was cute. Braden found it on Pinterest as a kid's cake. A little fence of KitKats adhered to the side of a simple chocolate cake. Inside the fence, was a field of brightly colored M&Ms. The Pinterest cake had pigs in the field as if the whole cake was a big pig pen, but we were going simple for Iain's graduation party.

"What I don't understand," I continued, "is why we're going to Iain's graduation in the first place. Didn't you guys only date for like a month?"

"Eh, six weeks" Braden corrected. "I stay friends with people I date. I might not be into Iain, but he's a nice guy."

"Mmhmm, still weird." I teased. Again, Braden was my complete opposite. Throughout our years rooming together, if I brought a guy home and it didn't work out, he might well have fallen off the face of the earth. A clean break. Braden on the other hand, was friends with everyone. Steady and calm, in both work ethic and friendship. It's what I liked about him then, and even to the day I'm writing this. It's what everyone likes about Braden.

"Plus I think his roommate's straight..." he added in a singsongy voice. He had been trying on the new voice every once in a while these last few weeks as he'd joined the Pride club on campus. He had come out as gay before I met him, but not too much earlier. He was still finding his own voice (as we all were at that age). The fake voice I could forgive, but I crinkled my nose at the sentiment.

His roommate's straight? So what. I wasn't in the mood for dating.

Once the cake was completely assembled, we needed the finishing touch; a Lumberjack ribbon. Braden knelt down and tied the bow. It looked awful against the rainbow-colored M&M's, but I didn't have the heart to say anything.

"I think that works!" Braden announced, wiping his hands on his jeans. "I'm gonna go get ready–"

SLAM - BANG! - CRAAAASH!

Virginia, my new gray cat darted out of the kitchen in a blur. She had been sitting on her favorite perch on top of the fridge as we were decorating.

My eyes widened.

The cake.

The cake Braden had been working on for two days lay splattered across the floor. m&m shockwaves were spread across the kitchen into the living room behind us.

"VIRGINIA!" I shouted, but she had already hidden herself in her favorite spot under my bed.

We stared at the mess open-mouthed for several seconds, taking in the mess. The plate we had been decorating on wobbled on the linoleum from the momentum of the fall. The *wub wub wub* of each orbit slowed down with each turn until finally coming slowing to a stop.

I turned to Braden, mortified by what my cat had done to all his hard work. "I'm *so* sorry." My voice was shaking, barely strong enough to muster the words louder than a whisper, "I didn't even think she'd jump on it. I –"

Braden's sigh interrupted me. He rubbed at his face. "It's okay, it's not your fault."

But his expression said it all. His hands remained glued to his face. He was frozen. We both were.

M&Ms littered the kitchen floor. Some even found their way into the living room. We'd be finding them for weeks! The cake was unsalvageable. Half of the KitKats were broken. The cake itself was split in two and glued to the floor with icing.

I didn't dare make the first move.

Finally, Braden grabbed the cake. In one ungraceful motion, slupped it into the garbage. The sound of cake hitting the plastic bottom of the trash can sealed its fate. Goodbye, cake.

"I guess I'll just pick up some rum and cookies from Trader Joe's?" Braden asked, as though I'd ever disagree with him after this mistake.

"Great idea!" I said. I was sure he needed a few minutes away from the mess. Moreso, he probably needed a few minutes away from me for causing it.

"Let me give you money," I added, "I'll clean this up and then we can head out." With that, I pulled out my wallet, giving him considerably more cash than was needed. He didn't protest.

* * *

That evening, we knocked on Iain's apartment door with our sad Trader Joe's bag in tow. We stood in silence. Neither of us could bring ourselves to discuss *The Incident*, but there was nothing else to say.

Finally, Iain's roommate opened the door. I recognized him, but couldn't quite place where.

We stepped into the apartment.

"Hey!" the roommate greeted, pointing a finger gun at Braden "Braden, right?"

"Yep, Braden! Derek?"

"Yeah, come on in, it's cold."

Derek grabbed the bag from Braden as we entered the apartment. "This is my roommate, Rhonwyn."

"Oh yeah, I remember, I went to your birthday party!"

"That's right!" – I knew I had seen him from somewhere.

We joined the rest of the party who were setting up a board game in the living room.

"Here, Rhonwyn, sit next to Derek," Iain instructed, "no reason at all."

Iain exchanged a mischievous look with his roommate. I wondered what they might have talked about to warrant the look. *Was he trying to set Derek up with me?*

Curious, I obliged, taking a spot on the carpet between the two friends. Iain and Derek took turns explaining the rules of the Quelf.

I was intrigued by the odd pair. Physically, they looked like they could be brothers, with sandy brown hair, pale skin, and gray eyes. But their demeanors and interactions complimented each other. Iain was bundled up for the Flagstaff weather with a fuzzy jacket and beanie hat. Meanwhile, Derek sported athletic shorts and a t-shirt.

The two talked over each other as they pulled out the pieces, but I could quickly gather it was simple enough. Players move around the board, drawing cards that instruct them to perform various absurd tasks.

The added house rules (of course) were to drink any time you had to move back a space, or two drinks if you refer to anyone by their real name rather than that of their character.

"Henceforth, I am Mr. Lugnut!" Derek claimed his ridiculous game piece proudly.

Iain claimed Batbileg Chinzorig, and Braden took The Platypus.

Queen Spatula seemed a far better choice than Mrs. Picklefeather, so I grabbed her character quickly.

I watched with keen interest as Derek and Iain delved into the goofy game. Iain rolled first. He drew a card and placed it back in the pile.

"Arr, me turn be done, mateys!" Iain growled and squinted an eye.

"Bloody Pirate." Derek feigned a British accent.

"A brave soul must roll a mighty six for my speech to not sound like a scallywag."

I was up next. Rolling a 4, I moved Queen Spatula up to her spot on the board and took my card.

A Challenge of The Arts: You and the player seated across from you must engage in a drawing competition. Set the timer. Using your non-dominant hands, create an image of a cowboy riding a hotdog. The remaining players will vote on a winner. The loser moves back one space.

I was up against Braden. We turned the sand timer over and drew our little cowboys. Now, I've always been competitive, so I was FOCUSED on winning against my roommate. Still, I couldn't help but feel Derek's eyes on me as I drew my little character. My cheeks began to turn red.

The sand emptied from the top of the timer. *Time's up.*

We revealed our little cowboy hotdog riders.

"Avast! Your efforts may be mighty, cap'n, but I must vote for the lass," said Iain. Victory."

I was the unquestioned winner of the round.

Braden stuck a tongue out at me. He took a drink, but he didn't have to move back a space. His turn hadn't come around yet, so he was still at the start.

Derek rolled a 6, bringing his game piece two spaces ahead of mine and freeing Iain of his piracy.

He grinned widely and stood up, offering a hand out with a bow.

"May I have this dance?"

Derek took my waist and we waltzed clumsily around the crowded living room. I hated dancing, but this was dramatic enough that it was all good fun.

Returning to the game after our dance, Derek made intense eye contact with the board. Knowing I was looking at him, he pushed his card toward me so that I could read it.

Slow dance with a player of your choice.

Your choice. I thought. My skin prickled as I noticed the second play of the evening. Something was brewing here.

The game progressed with ridiculous outfits and quick competitions. We were all feeling the buzz as our pieces moved around the board. Braden came back from behind claiming first place and ending round one.

* * *

"I don't know if you two should walk back tonight," suggested Iain as the party continued into the wee hours of the morning, "it's just so late, and you're more than welcome to stay here."

Derek yawned "I'm getting pretty tired myself."

"No more hitting on Rhonwyn!" Iain teased. "I know your plays."

"I'm not making a play!" Derek protested "I'm just actually tired. In fact, Rhonwyn, would you like to sleep in my bed? I will take the couch downstairs."

"Actually that would be great" I admitted, exhausted, and a little bit curious.

Derek escorted me through the hallway to his room. He kept a respectful distance from the door.

The hall was much calmer. Quiet. Music and our roommates' voices were all muffled by the stairs. It was the first time Derek and I were alone together.

I noticed his eyes were a light gray. Different than Iain's deep brown. In fact, looking at him in front of his bedroom, he didn't look like Iain at all. There was something sharper about his nose and ears.

He's pretty cute. I thought, but I didn't want to make any moves.

"Anyway this is me," he blurted out quickly, awkwardly rubbing the back of his scalp, "Bathroom's right over there. I'll be downstairs. Let me know if you need anything."

With that, he turned away quickly and scurried down the stairs.

I smiled at his awkwardness. It matched mine.

"Thanks!" I called back to him with a smile.

Alone. I thought. *Alone in a guy's room.*

And "guy's room" it was. I couldn't help but snoop on the bedroom of this new friend. I'd been in guys' dorms before, and this was no different. Of course, there was the classic "Why So Serious" poster of Heath Ledger's Joker. *Did every 21-year-old man own this?* On the bed, a forest green comforter had been loosely thrown across the top. He clearly "made an effort" in this action, as the sheets were completely un- tucked. I could tell he wasn't a bed-maker. And, true to "Guy's Room" form, there was literally zero additional furniture.

I inspected the built-in desk in the corner. A binder and two text- books were laid open on top of it. Under one of the textbooks was a scribbled drawing from a toddler. The mom had clearly labeled it "Happy Birthday Uncle D! Love, Jaxon."

Something about Derek being an uncle seemed so endearing. Not having siblings myself, this seemed like such a sweet aspect to this messy, awkward guy.

I looked under the desk.

I was relieved to see lots of books. He had a wide range of topics from *The Samarillian* to *The Conquest of Gaul* to *Ancient Animals: The Plesiosaur* stacked on the floor.

"Don't sleep with boys who don't have books," – that was a rule Mariah and I fiercely lived by.

Behind all the books sat a large collection of rocks. They ranged in size from shoeboxes of tiny rocks to small boulders about the size of bowling balls.

I know your plays. Iain had teased Derek just before bed. I wondered if there was more to this guy. *How many girls did he bring back here?* And, more pressing, *I wonder if he wants to bring me back here.*

I pulled out my phone to text my friend downstairs;

BRADEN

So what do we know about Derek?

Ha. Knew it.

Mix Batter

Choose Your Own Adventure

I've always been a firm believer that everyone should work in customer service at least once in their life. I've been subscribing to that ideology since I was 16 years old–just six months into my first job at Paradise Bakery. Between Paradise, Sodexo Campus Dining, and Sam's Club in my High School and College days, I thought graduation in 2013 meant I was done with all that. *I'd served my time – five years of it!* From my experiences, I'd learned how to be a polite customer and a good tipper, but now was the time to get into an actual office. A "real world" job.

Unfortunately, while the recession was waning, it hadn't completely come to a close. There were no jobs out there. Somehow, I'd become the stereotypical college graduate who clutched onto their English degree while working at Starbucks and living with Mom and Dad. *Millennials, am I right?*

My parents moved back to St. Louis during my time at NAU, so moving back home to me actually meant moving *back home.* As in back to my hometown. It was a new house for Mom and Dad, but I was back in the city I'd called home until middle school. The last time any of my Missouri friends saw me, I was a gangly 7th grader. They had no idea that I'd fared somewhat reasonably in High School and eventually found footing in college. To them, in the blink of an eye, the awkward girl who sat next to them in math was the Barista serving them their *$6*

Triple Venti Oat Milk Caramel Macchiato with Two Extra Pumps. Oh, how the mediocre had fallen further.

It was only a matter of time before *it happened.* The bell at the top of our Starbucks jingled, and in walked none other than *Alyssa Czerenko-Greer,* former 7th-grade Volleyball star and most popular girl at Barnwell Middle.

I had just turned 22 years old. It shouldn't have bothered me to see Alyssa, but boy, did it ever. She looked professional, with steamed slacks and a ruffled blouse. She looked *older.* Of course, we were about the same age, both technical adults, but Alyssa Czerenko-Greer looked like she had a cubicle and a real office job. She was an adult. I was serving coffee.

"Excuse me." Alyssa was in front of me, staring at me with her crystal blue, perfectly-lined eyes. "I'd like to order." It was clear from the politeness in her voice that she didn't recognize me.

Dagger-in-gut. *Why was that worse?*

"Hi, sorry yes–" Shaking my head to return to reality, I muttered out the script; "Hi, Welcome to Starbucks, what can I get for you?"

"Ummm... get me a large cinnamon dolce latte with an extra shot and non-fat milk." The demand-order. The dagger twists. "Oh and a Cinnamon Coffee Cake."

"Sure thing. Double Venti Non-fat Cinnamon Dolce Latte, and a Coffee Cake." I repeated in Starbucks Jargon as I wrote the order on the cup. Pausing to add, "Name?" – I wasn't going to let her know I knew her.

"Alyssa...also? You said that kind of weird. I want an extra shot." Alyssa's perfectly manicured index finger gestured toward the cup. I noticed the hand it was attached to and the GIANT diamond ring. She was engaged.

Great, I thought. *Adult job and an engagement. This is just great.*

A sigh escaped my typically believable customer service voice, "There's like an order you have to say it in," I explained, "A double just means you want an extra shot." I placed the empty cup on the counter next to me. "That'll be 11 dollars and twenty-six cents."

Alyssa's designer purse thudded on the counter in front of me. "Oh let me see I have cash" Alyssa pulled out five singles and a quarter. "Shoot, it looks like I don't have a penny." she narrated, narrowing her eyes onto the Tip Jar between us. She reached her diamond-laden hand into the tip jar for the extra cent, whispering, "You don't mind, do you? Just a penny."

"Not a problem," I said through gritted teeth.

After Alyssa's Coffee Cake and Double Venti Non-fat Cinnamon Dolce Latte were both in her hands, I let my boss know that I was going on my fifteen. I slouched at my usual corner table, fuming with envy as Alyssa Czerenko-Greer plunged her teeth into her coffee cake.

Starbucks' website describes their Cinnamon Coffee cake as a "Buttery, moist, coffee cake swirled with a cinnamon-sugar blend and finished with a crunchy streusel topping." Made with the highest quality ingredients (or it better be, priced at a whopping $5.79) the Starbucks Cinnamon Coffee Cake is a true indulgence like no other. The cinnamon-sugar blend swirls throughout the cake, providing a sweet and spicy flavor that perfectly complements the rich coffee undertones.

I'd eaten it before. It's fine.

I pulled out my phone, mentally exhausted from work and envy.

Gmail - 2 Missed Emails

Hope surged through my body with a jolt pulling me out of the restaurant. I tapped on the email app.

From: Charles Green
Subject: RE: Green & Snyder Application

Dear Rhonwyn,
My colleague Josh and I were very impressed with your resume and we'd love for you to come in to meet with the partners. Is there any chance you can come in this Saturday for an interview? We'd like to get someone in the role quickly.

-Charlie

Charles Green, JD
Partner, Green & Snyder

I opened the next one.

From: mealzthathealz@gmail.com
Subject: Interview Wednesday?

I just had a chance to review your application. RU free sometime this week for an interview?

My heart felt like it was beating a million miles a minute. I was out. I could *feel* it. I had to supply writing samples for both of these jobs, so if they liked my samples, an interview was just a formality. Anxiety would not allow me to reply to those emails within the confines of my fifteen-minute break, but I clocked back in. I was beaming.

* * *

Sometimes in life, you don't get to choose your own adventure. You're stuck living with your parents and working at a Starbucks because money exists, and there's no other option. That's why you had to join me in a dingy Starbucks uniform taking Alyssa Czerenko-Greer's order, (Remember, I told you I was a firm believer you have to serve your time in service. Gotta serve your time in this book, too). But other times, you *can* choose, and particularly during your early twenties, these small choices can often be the choices that set the course for where you're going to end up.

Now, at the precipice of these two interviews, I'm going to let you Choose Your Own Adventure. In reality, I went to both Green & Snyder and Mealz That Healz, but honestly this chapter would be ungodly long if you read through both interviews. So, if you were a twenty-something, let's see where you'd end up – Cozy Cubicle, or left for dead on the side of a highway. (I'M JOKING...kind of).

Rhonwyn has two interviews this week. Which one is she on the way to now?

Mealz That Healz	Green & Snyder
Continue reading on page 111	Skip to page 120

The Mealz that Healz executive assistant interview was at 1659 Baker's Street in Ladue. Since moving back to Missouri, I'd learned that Ladue was considered the "rich" part of town. I imagined something like Scottsdale, AZ with tidy shops and restaurants lining the main roads, and enormous McMansions looking over from a distance. Fancy ones like Mariah's house in High School, with perfectly manicured lawns and ornate garage doors. (Rich people seem to have fancier garage doors, right? Like there's a level of richness in which you start caring about what the door your cars use looks like.) I pictured Mealz that Healz being in a fancy office park or above one of those tidy shops.

As the GPS guided me through the neighborhoods of Ladue, I found that my idea of their houses was 100% correct, including the garage doors. However, this being Missouri, there were several more tacky lawn sculptures of lions or cherubs. Ladue wasn't embracing the modern era like Scottsdale. To me, it felt more like "new money," but still *deeply Midwest.*

"You have arrived." the lady in my GPS announced.

I picked the phone back up. *I'm still in the middle of the neighborhood.* I thought to myself while I confirmed the address I'd printed out from the email.

1659 Baker's Street. Ladue, Missouri.

Looking back up, this was definitely the right spot, but there wasn't a store in sight. Instead, I took in the facade of the stone brick house that had to be about 3,500 square feet. Fancy garage door and all.

I was confused. Fancy as it was, this was a *residence*, not a business address.

My car inched forward as I let off the brake, just a hair. *Imagine if I'm in the wrong place.* I thought. *I will miss my interview AND have to knock on someone's door and explain that for some reason I thought I had an interview...at their house?*

I looked at the clock: 10:48. The interview was at 11. I had time to walk a bit. Fearing the awkward conversation I was going to have to endure, I parked my car about a block up the street. For some reason this sense of control made me feel more comfortable about my impending social gaffe.

TAP-TAP-TAP

I knew from Mariah's house growing up that you aren't actually supposed to use rich people's fancy door knockers. Instead, I gently knocked on the door the normal way with my knuckles.

A middle-aged man in basketball shorts and a plain black T-shirt opened the door. By the look of his gray stubble, I'd guessed it'd been at least a day or two since his last shave, though his hair was quite gelled and tidy. As he opened the door further, I noticed he was joined by a big German Shepherd with *German-Shepherd teeth*. The dog's nails scraped against the floor as she tried to make her way to me. The man restrained her.

"DOWN STELLA!" he commanded, pulling the door open further to allow me to slide in past the pair of them.

Once we were settled in the foyer with the door closed, he let go of Stella's harness. I gently acknowledged the dog as she sniffed my pants, leaving behind awkward wet nose marks on my thighs. *God just please don't sniff my crotch*, I implored her internally.

"Hey you must be Rhonwyn," he said, holding out a hand.

Feeling a sense of familiarity with social norms inside of all the chaos, I took his hand with a firm but-not-harsh interview handshake. "Hi, yes, you're Mitchel?"

"Yes," he said, "great to meet you; SIT!"

Stella and I both straightened up at Mitchel's command, with Stella taking an added beat to obediently sit down.

"The *dog*," Mitchel added, laughing lightly. "But actually, you too. Come on in, have a seat at the island where I have my laptop set up. I'll put her in her kennel."

I made my way toward the huge granite island and pulled out a barstool. It was surprisingly heavy.

"STELLA; KENNEL!" Mitchel barked.

I jumped at the command.

Mitchel smiled at me with pride. There's something about men being able to successfully train a dog that makes them feel powerful.

I smiled politely at my interviewer and took a seat.

While Mitchel fiddled with the cage lock, I flipped through my resume and notes one last time, putting a pen on top of my folder so I could take any necessary notes.

Mitchel returned to the kitchen with a confident stride in his step.

"So where did you park?" he asked, taking a seat at the kitchen island behind his laptop.

"Oh, Just a little up the street. I wasn't sure if I had the right place, so..." I trailed off, feeling like that was more smalltalk than anything.

"Ah yeah, I see. If you get the job, it's no problem to park in the driveway. All my drivers do it so you can too."

"Thanks. Noted." I said

"So you had *the* top WPM speed on my typing test, which is awesome. Tell me about yourself. What do you do?"

I gave my elevator pitch explaining that I had absolutely zero office job experience, but that I'd worked before and learned many important aspects of working from Sam's Club and Paradise Bakery. I'd upsold customers into credit cards. I majored in English, and really just want to find a job that allows me to write in any capacity – marketing copy, emails, etc.

Mitchel's wide head rested in his right hand as I continued on. He seemed to be actively listening, or at least doing a good job of pretending he was. That is until his next question.

"What's that smell?" he finally asked at the end of my answer.

Blood rushed to my cheeks as I paused to think of a reply, "Um, oh it might be my perfume, I'm sorry. I work at Starbucks now, so maybe I overdo it–"

"No, it's okay. It's great actually. You smell like a *fairy princess.*"

What an odd comment Rhonwyn has received. What would you think of it?

<table>
<tr><td>RED FLAG. Turn around.</td><td>Nah, It's just awkward.</td></tr>
<tr><td>Continue reading on page 115</td><td>Skip to page 116</td></tr>
</table>

I shifted in my chair a bit. I'm bad enough at compliments, *really* bad at creepy.

I took an inventory of the room while I thought of a response. It was normal – a normal living room with two Big Boy chairs. It was clearly a bachelor pad, but it was a bachelor pad someone had invested in. He had money, so I trusted the Mealz That Healz business was at least partially successful, despite its awful name.

Stella snoozed in her kennel. She was secured.

Behind me, the door to the basement was slightly ajar. *What if there's a trio of naked girls my age chained in the basement? In dog kennels just like Stella.*

I banished the intrusive thought from my head. *Okay, Rhonwyn, don't let your imagination run wild. Focus on the interview for fuck's sake. It's an interview. A quirky one, but what's wrong with a slightly creepy boss compared to a series of Alyssa Czerenko-Greers before they have their morning coffee?*

Truly, I did think about leaving. But I decided to stay.

Sorry, you don't get a choice.

Continue reading on the next page

"Haha," I breathed a false laugh.

He returned with a far more confident chuckle "Ha! I kid, I kid. That's not this kind of ad. I don't think it was anyway? I do have one of those out... if you're interested."

My mind immediately ran to those "Personal Secretary" ads I'd seen on Craigslist in my job hunting. You know the ones--less of a job ad, and more of a man playing out some desk sex fantasy. I wondered if he wrote one of those ads I'd scrolled past.

"Anyway–" Mitchel said, pulling out a big document that looked like it had been printed on one of the old printers with strips on the edges.

I smiled politely, not having an answer to his "other ad."

"So I have a test I give all of my employees," he continued professionally, "It's called the Jenkin's Exam – are you familiar with it?"

I admitted I hadn't heard of it.

"Basically just a 10-minute SAT seeing how much you use logic to solve problems. Here, you can take it in my office. It won't be too long."

What should Rhonwyn do next?

<table>
<tr><td>Seems Standard Enough</td><td>RED FLAG, DON'T TELL ME YOU'RE ACTUALLY CONSIDERING GOING IN HIS OFFICE IN HIS HOME. JESUS, WHAT'S WRONG WITH YOU?</td></tr>
<tr><td>Continue reading on page 117</td><td>Skip to page 119</td></tr>
</table>

Mitchel set me up at his desk in a small converted laundry room. There was one window about the size of a shoebox. It was too small for someone to crawl out of, say if that person were to find themselves locked in that room. But I'd been given exams at offices before. Again, I reassured myself *it's just a quirky interview.*

"Mind if I close this?" Mitchel asked, pulling the door closed. "I just want to let Stella out for a bit."

Behind Mitchel's wide form, I could see the entire kitchen, including my purse, hanging on the edge of the chair I'd been sitting on.

Jesus, is my phone in there?

Feeling another pang of uncertainty, I moved my hand to my pocket. I relaxed when I confirmed my phone was with me, not in the purse out of reach.

I nodded in agreement to Mitchel's initial question. He closed the door. The latch echoed through the small room.

My heart was thumping through my chest. *I could easily be raped or killed right now. Or both. Probably both. This is the beginning of a Law and Order SVU.*

The doorknob glowed back at me, begging me to test if it was locked.

I didn't budge. Instead, I turned around and opened the paper. *It was just a test.* I assured myself. *Just a test.*

As I answered math questions considering the birth order of septuplets based upon a series of clues, I heard a knock on the door outside.

"Nathan!" I heard Mitchel through the thick wood of the door. "Good to see you. I'm in an interview right now. Actually, come meet her, I think you might be working with her soon."

Two sets of footsteps approached the door. My anxiety was through the roof. *Were they going to abduct me? And god dammit, who is the oldest septuplet again? Was Suzette born before Klaudia? I'm not going to finish the test in time.*

Nathan and Mitchel opened the door, and my anxiety melted. Nathan was dressed head to toe in a "Meals with Wheels" Uniform. He was a delivery driver. He worked for this established company.

I chatted with the men, kicking myself for worrying about my safety during something as important as an interview.

After Nathan reloaded his jeep with packaged food, I turned back to Mitchel. He had the results of my test

In his words, "You're an average bear. I'm smarter than the average bear. But I can work with an Average bear."

Aside from the creepy comments, Mitchel never actually did anything inappropriate, but I had put myself in a dangerous situation in that interview.

Mitchel couldn't have been more right. That night, I was a very, very, very, dumb bear.

Where to next?

Rhonwyn, I'd love to see you do better.	I'm literally done. At least tell me you didn't work for him.
Skip to page 122	Skip to page 125

▶▶▶▶▶ - I know! I know, I know. I know what you're thinking.

But, consider where *you* are in *your* life now as you're reading this chapter. Maybe you have an okay job. It probably demands a lot mentally, and you're feeling some burnout. Valid. But you can buy drinks after work and not feel like you won't make next month's car payment.

Or, maybe you *are* working at Starbucks like I was, and you're on your feet on tile floors all day long, and you only make $7.25 an hour. Meaning it takes you an HOUR of work to earn the exact cost that some of your customers drink in one latte. It sucks. I get it.

It's really easy to sit back and see the red flags if you haven't worked in customer service in your life. (Again back to my point at the beginning of this chapter).

When you're an exhausted, 22-year-old, feeling like you wasted four years on an English degree, you can take a risk. Short of literally being sex trafficked, maybe a boss that hits on you isn't the worst thing. It'll be good resume fodder if you can stick it out for a year. You just need a foot in the door.

At least, that's how I felt.

Sorry, you don't get a choice.

Skip back up to page 117

I gave myself a solid 40 minutes to arrive at Green & Snyder Law Firm for my interview. It was a Saturday, which was odd for an office job, but it was an *office*, which was a vast improvement from the interview prior.

With the extra time, I called Danielle. Despite moving back to St. Louis, our phone call routine was the closest we could do to rekindling our friendship. Getting schedules to actually line up was impossible.

"Hey, what's up?" I could tell Danielle was crafting from the sound of her phone. It must have been on the table in front of her.

"Oh just sitting in the parking lot before my interview!"

"Nice! Didn't you just have one?"

"Yeah, I had two this week. The first one was weird. I ended up in some room at a guy's house. So I'm looking forward to this office one–"

"What? A room?"

"Nothing weird. Haha, I ended up in some tiny room to take a test. And the whole interview was at his house, but I think I did well over-all. He said I had the best typing speed of all his applicants, which is important for this job–"

"Yeah," Danielle interrupted, "I'm going to need you to go back to what you were saying about being in a room in his house. You didn't... did you sleep with him?"

"Oh my god, no! But I actually got the septuplet answer correct. I wasn't sure if Suzette was the oldest.."

"Rhonwyn, you're trying to tell me about how well you answered math questions, but I'm over here like you should be glad you left that interview intact and aren't like..*missing*!"

"Okay yeah, it was kind of dumb, but you don't understand, you're in college still. There are NO jobs available. I have to get out of Starbucks."

"Bitch, I work at *McDonald's*. You can cry into coffee-smelling clothes while I scrub grease out of my face every night. Also, seriously, don't do a Craigslist interview at someone's house again, or at least have my dad go with you and wait in the car."

"Fine. Peptalk me though okay? My next interview is in 20 minutes."

"In an *office*?"

"Yes, in an *office*."

Do you want to hear more?

Sounds weird. Just go to your Interview.	Wait, what is this conversation about?
Continue reading on page 122	Skip back up to page 111

It was 8:50 a.m. With ten minutes to go, it was time to walk into the building. It was a brick building, by a pond, in an office park. Feeling pepped up (albeit a bit chastised) by Danielle, I pulled the door handle with confidence...

Shit. It didn't budge.

I pulled again, rattling the door a bit.

"Uhh," I said aloud. I looked around for a call button. Maybe it was one of those fancy buildings with a doorman. I didn't know how any of this worked. I didn't see any obvious signs of a call button, doorbell, anything.

The anxiety started to rise in my chest as I inched towards the glass door, hoping there might be someone inside that could catch my eye. But it was a Saturday, nobody was in except for my interviewers.

I pulled out my phone and dialed the number. The St. Louis Personal Injury Law Industry ran a fun marketing game in which every Firm had its own claim on a single-digit phone number. Brown and Crouppen was 314-222-2222. Schultz & Myers was 314-444-4444 and so on. I dialed in the digit. Luckily it wasn't 314-666-6666.

"Hello, thank you for calling Green & Snyder. I'm Marty, how can I help you." I could tell from the tone it was an answering service.

I explained the situation. Locked out of a Saturday morning interview. Marty was sympathetic, but couldn't do anything. He explained his notes go to the team on Monday morning.

"Sorry." Marty told me, "I'm just an answering service."

"Thanks, I guess," I said, bidding Marty goodbye at 9:01.

I had arrived at the parking lot 40 minutes early, but here I was, late to the office itself.

In desperation, I walked around the building. Maybe there's a back entrance?

My eyes welled up as I walked around the back of the building. There was a lovely cement picnic table overlooking another pond. I imagined the likes of Alyssa Czerenko-Greer taking their lunch breaks in warmer weather and watching young geese roam the pond.

It was 9:05. I sat on the bench, accepting defeat. I used the sleeve of my coat to wipe the snot off my nose. Even if I did get in at that point, what were the chances they'd offer a job to someone who shows up late to the interview?

I looked up, and in the distance, a car was pulling into the parking lot. Of course, someone would show up now. I figured I should at least go into the building to apologize to the interviewers. I stood up so I could follow them into the building.

A well-dressed woman got out of her car and walked briskly to the front door. I followed her in, thanking her as she held the door behind me. She turned right and I turned left. There it was, Etched in glass on the entrance to their suite. "Green & Snyder Law Firm. Personal Injury Lawyers on YOUR Side."

The receptionist's seat was empty when I entered the suite. It was Saturday, after all.

Deep voices mumbled in the distance behind the reception station. It must have been coming from one of the offices.

Two tall men walked briskly out of the office dressed in coats. They were ready to leave.

"How fucking rude is it for someone to not show up to an interview?" the taller of the two men complained, "Not even call–" He stopped himself when he saw me.

There they were, the two lawyers I'd seen on every billboard, and they were pissed that I stood them up.

"Hey" the lawyer I recognized from billboards as Green began, "We were uh..."

"Just talking about me?" I said with a smile and nothing to lose.

"Oh my god, I'm so embarrassed, I apologize–" He seemed to be genuinely more embarrassed about getting caught swearing than I was for being late.

"No, no, no it's okay," I assured him, "I couldn't get in because the door was locked–"

"Oh my god, it's Saturday!" the other lawyer, Snyder, realized my situation.

We mumbled through apologies, unsure of who made the worse error.

Snyder broke the awkwardness with an outstretched hand–a symbolic rewind of the past twenty minutes leading up to our very tardy interview. "Hi, I'm Josh."

"I'm Rhonwyn," I returned the handshake.

I nailed the interview.

Continue reading on the next page.

The next week at work, I bit into a Cinnamon Coffee Cake, letting crumbly streusel topping flood my mouth.

I received not one, but *TWO* job offers since that terrible shift with Alyssa Czerenko-Greer. I had to savor every minute. I knew that Coffee Cake would be one of the last free pastries of my Starbucks career. I wasn't too down about it; I knew I could buy myself one any time because *I* had just landed an office job.

I let Mitchel from Mealz that Healz know I could start in two weeks. One week if he might consider me for that "other" ad of his. (wink).

(I'M TOTALLY KIDDING!)

Thanks for reading. It's time to go to bed! How do you like to save your spot in a book?

I dogear the page.	Never ruin a book! Let me grab my bookmark.
Excellent. Please do this 16 times, rip the page, then burn the book. Then, head to Amazon and buy another copy of my book so you can finish reading. No reason. Thanks.	Nerd.

Easy Bake Oven, and Other ways that Cake Can Kill You

Mad Men was midway through their seventh season when I started my marketing career. Before my first day at Green & Snyder, Mad Men had been my *only* introduction to marketing. Naturally, it was an awful example to base my career off of.

First, I was in digital marketing, which didn't even exist at Mad Men's 1960's agency, Sterling Cooper.

Second, Green & Snyder was a personal injury law firm, not an agency. I wasn't peddling something fun like lipstick or coffee. I was selling the firm you're supposed to hire after an accident or tragedy ruins your life.

That being said, I was fortunate. We were well past the years of women like Peggy Olsen being not given a seat at the table to share marketing ideas of her own. To the contrary; despite being fresh out of college, the partners gave me the freedom and confidence to explore and learn about the relatively young industry of digital marketing on my own. As long as I was bringing people to the website and getting our keywords ranking on Google's search pages, I was free to my own devices.

By 2015, I was growing confident in my new role. I had a lot to learn, but I *loved* learning it. I often quipped that I put the "chase" in "ambulance chaser."

It was my job to cultivate a list of leads for personal injury lawyers. This was a challenge in marketing as you never could know when someone was going to need a lawyer. Also, paradoxically, we didn't necessarily *want* our followers to need to call us. This is where SEO (Search Engine Optimization) came into play.

To grossly oversimplify SEO at the time, Google looked at website structure, titles, web page keywords, and popularity of your page to determine the order it presented search results. If Google favored your website, they pushed your search rank up for common search phrases. In the instance of personal injury law, our phrases had something to do with car accidents or workplace injuries.

How did we get the popularity of visits up on Green & Snyder pages? Mostly by blogging. Topics involving cars, workplace safety equipment, and so on. You know, preventing the injury, while still talking about it enough to boost SEO.

Here's the problem; no one wants to casually read about a dashboard injury called Chondromalacia of the Medial Femoral Condyle. They also won't read a blog about what to do when your insurance denies your claim because the other driver was uninsured, blah blah blah. That's *boring!*

People are *sick.* People want *blood.* They want fire and freak accidents. They want to know how many children had to have their hands amputated because they got stuck in an Easy Bake Oven!

Enter *Clickbait.* (Oh how 2015 was an era of clickbait!) I wrote boring blogs, to be sure. "Chondromalacia of the Medial Femoral Condyle" was the meat and potatoes to get us clients who actually needed help. I also *had* to write the wild freak accident blogs to get the clicks. (To help the SEO, of course.) Let me tell you, I learned a LOT of ways you can die in a freak accident. And I mean a LOT.

So for this chapter, instead of any particular story revolving around cake, I thought it would be fun to stretch out my old blog writing muscles by putting together some freak accidents involving cake.

Guys, Gals, Non-Binary Gender Pals... (Who am I kidding? I'm in marketing. I know my target demo for this book.) *Ladies...* For your reading pleasure, I present to you:

EASY BAKE OVEN, AND OTHER WAYS THAT CAKE CAN KILL YOU.

1. Easy Bake Oven

No, Easy Bake Oven hasn't actually killed a kid yet (I'm not apologizing for the clickbait chapter title). However, back in 2007, Hasbro had to recall their Easy Bake Oven Model number 65805 after 249 reports of burn injuries. No joke!

For those of you who had a bad childhood and never got to bake on an Easy Bake Oven, the toy comes with these little powder packets that you can mix with water and bake under a heat lamp for a set amount of time. To get the cake into the oven, there's a tiny slot on the side (as opposed to opening it wide like an actual oven. Hasbro had enough forethought for not doing that one). Well, turns out that kids were sticking their little fingers into the slot rather than using the tool to pull the cakes out, and burning their skin against the heat lamp. These weren't small burns either. There was one report of a five-year-old who had to have her finger partially amputated due to the severity of the burn! Sheesh!

Anyway, apparently the toys had to be recalled for repair, and they've made safety updates now that don't even have the heat lamp in question. I haven't done a ton of research, so I'm not sure how the "cake" gets baked anymore without the heat lamp, but that's neither here nor there.

Seriously, watch your kids around those things.

2. Contracting Hepatitis A from a Bakery

This one didn't specifically have anything to do with cake, but I included it because it *could*. You get Hepatitis A from eating contaminated food as it is transmitted through a fecal-oral route (Read: Eating Someone's Shit). There have been cases in which people died after eating contaminated food at a restaurant.

Hear me out - in theory, an infected cake decorator doesn't wash their hands after using the bathroom, goes back to their work with no gloves, and finishes the piping work. The decorator gets brought out to a lovely wedding shared by many many wedding guests.

How do you know if you're infected? Apparently, you don't show symptoms until about 15-50 days after infection. (That's good news if our Bride and Groom ended up going on a honeymoon shortly after their wedding. Potentially bad news for anyone who honeymooned near them). Some people don't have symptoms at all. According to the CDC, others can have some combination of stomach problems, fever, dark urine, light stools, and jaundice. If you're immunocompromised though, Hepatitis A can really take you down. It kills about 7,000 people a year!

3. Distracted Driving - Distractions aren't always Technology

Okay, this one I actually learned from writing a Green & Snyder blog. You know how commercials tout that distracted driving accounts for 10% of all auto accidents? Get this; Distracted driving doesn't necessarily mean you're texting or talking on the phone. (Or at least it didn't. I'm going off of 2015 data here).

When you look at the breakdown, they categorize any distraction as distracted driving. Turning up the radio. Reaching down to pick something out of your purse. Putting makeup on. Heck, even "zoning out" is categorized as distracted driving.

Here's my cake death scenario; you're driving your car home from a kid's birthday party and you brought home a Tupperware container of extra cake because the other kid's mom's on a diet or something. Your kids are strapped in their boosters in the back seat, and you foolishly put the cake between them. Your oldest grabs it. Starts eating. Well, it's almost dinner time so you don't want them spoiling it. You tell them to put it away, but they're not going to listen, so you reach your arm in the back to grab the container.

BAM! - your SUV slams straight into the back of a pickup truck. You're at fault because you were distracted by cake.

4. Diabetic Ketoacidosis

Yes, you can die from too much cake. I mean, probably not *you*. But if you have diabetes, it's possible. Let me introduce Diabetic Ketoacidosis. DKA develops when there is a lack of insulin, leading to a buildup of glucose in the blood. The cells and tissues aren't getting the fuel they need, so the liver responds by releasing stored glucose, which further increases glucose levels.

If there isn't enough insulin, the body tries to cope by increasing urination and burning fat as an alternate fuel source. This leads to the formation of ketone bodies, which can signal trouble when combined with high blood glucose and a lack of insulin. DKA is more likely to occur in people with type 1 diabetes, but anyone with diabetes can develop it. Strictly speaking, you're more likely to develop DKA due to improperly medicating, missing some insulin doses, or drinking alcohol excessively while taking insulin. But you know what, you can technically just throw off your levels with a TON of cake.

Feeling short of breath, urinating a lot, excessively thirsty? Check your urine for ketones. You can get a keystone strip test without a prescription at the drugstore.

5. *Being Crushed to Death in a Trash Compactor*

Crush injuries are in the top five most common workplace injuries, and they have catastrophic, sometimes fatal results. When your body part is caught, crushed, pinched, or compressed, the inside suffers severe damage. So if we're talking about an arm, then you might need it amputated. If we're talking about your torso, then there's potential for organ damage and death.

If you work at one of those warehouse grocery stores, you probably have an onsite trash compactor. We had one when I worked at Sam's Club. In the bakery, we donated most of the bread to a nearby soup kitchen. We'd fill boxes and boxes of day-old bread (not expired, but we baked fresh) and leave it on a pallet in the back room for the soup kitchen to pick up. That said, some of the *cakes* went to waste. For one, there wasn't as much of a need for cake as there was for bread. If the soup kitchen had to choose, they'd choose bread. Secondly, we would sell the cake up until the sell-by date. If the sell-by date passes, you can't donate it. Do you see where I'm going with all this cake? You guessed it; the trash compactor.

This was an absolutely disgusting task. Next to the trash compactor was a 7' tall wood 2x4. Sharpied on the front was a line with an arrow at each end. One side was labeled "handle side" and the other, "nasty side." After you put the trash in the compactor, you hold the handle side and use the nasty side to move it down. Obviously, you don't start the machine while you're doing this. But...what if someone did?

I was fortunate to never have a crush injury or get sucked into a trash compactor during my time at Sam's Club, but every once in a while, you see it in the news cycle. One example, in 2013, a man was killed by a trash compactor while searching for his cell phone that he believed he accidentally dropped inside it. When he was searching, an automatic sensor triggered the compactor to run, trapping him inside.

It happens all the time. Hundreds of people were maimed or killed in industrial trash compactors. And that's why there's worker's comp!

6. *Moldy Cake*

We talked about Hepatitis-A-infected cake already, but what about really really old cake? You know how couples always save their wedding cake in the freezer for a year to eat on their anniversary? (Yeah, that's gross, I didn't do that either. And if you did, I don't think we can be friends anymore.)

But let's say you did save your cake for a year. If you improperly stored your cake, or left it out a long time before you put it in the freezer, it's not going to be in great shape. You could potentially pull out a moldy cake at your one-year anniversary.

Mold isn't likely to kill you, but it could make you very sick from mycotoxins–toxic chemicals that mold can produce. Depending on how much you eat and how healthy you are, it could lead to nausea or vomiting, liver disease, and even death.

If you or a loved one has ever been killed or injured by a cake or other baked goods, you may be entitled to compensation. For a free, no-obligation consultation, call us at... Oh, wait. Sorry, old habits die hard.

* * *

Anyway, for years I tapped into my inner hypochondriac. If I wasn't buying ketone strips over the counter knowing full well I didn't have diabetes, I was typing out blogs about what could potentially kill you at any given moment, or how an insurance company can (and will) try to take advantage of your family after something killed you.

The subject matter was interesting, to say the least. But most importantly, I learned a lot from my first office job. I learned Google Analytics like the back of my hand. I learned how to pull complex logic lists from databases, and how to advertise on social media. I also learned the intangibles like when and when not to hit "reply all" on an email, exactly how many drinks to imbibe at an office party, and that when you work in digital marketing, everyone thinks that you just play on social media all day.

I'm not in personal injury law marketing anymore, but I'm a marketer through and through. In a book about my life, I had to find a way to pay tribute to the career that I've chosen for myself, and how it all started with two kind bosses who let me blog my heart out about freak accidents.

Our Wedding Cake

When I started to write this book, I had Summer, 2017 inked in immediately. Obviously. Wedding Cake. *My wedding cake.* This is going to have to go in here somewhere. But so much happens on a wedding day that I had no idea where to start. Worlds collide on your wedding day. Of course, you have your coworkers, college friends, high school friends, family, and so on. Then there's your partner's coworkers, college friends, high school friends, family, and so on.

When you're as socially anxious as I am, you chameleon yourself to your circumstances. Change aspects of your personality to match. And I don't even just mean not swearing around Grandma and in the office. For me, I've always changed patterns of speech, talked about different preferences, and even made different facial expressions, depending on what group of people I'm with. I don't like to be put on the spot, so I desperately try to match and blend in. Here's the problem – on a wedding day, you can't do that. You're only one person, so there's no changing yourself to fit the mold. It's your wedding day. You and your partner make the mold.

This all came to a head in the ceremony itself–Derek and I aren't religious, so it was important to us that we didn't have any "blessings" or "prayers" from our officiant. But being eager to please and blend, I wanted to give my guests an outlet for prayer. Our officiant suggested a ring-warming ceremony. It's a Celtic tradition in which the couples' rings are attached to a string and then the rings are passed from guest to guest, snaking in and out of each row of chairs. As the rings are passed to you, you take them in your hands to give the rings good vibes, prayers, blessings, or a quick "good luck." The string stays behind, eventually linking everyone together. *Cute right*? I thought it was...

It checked all the boxes; A place for Nana Cookie to pray (check). Means of keeping prayers out of the officiant's mouth (check). Great for pictures (check). Bonus points–distracting enough that I felt less pressure of all eyes on me during our vows (check).

Our mistake, however, was assuming our guests to be far more crafty than they actually were. I mean, come on guys, out of the 115 of you, not one could figure out how to pull yarn from the center of the skein?

I'm getting ahead of myself. Let me rewind...

When the day of the wedding arrived, my brides-people and I were stationed out of sight in the gift shop of the Flagstaff Arboretum. We established at the rehearsal that the gift shop was the best place for me to hide before the outdoor wedding. I could see Derek and the guests through the window, but they couldn't see me.

As 3:00 inched closer, I peered through the window. Derek talking to his sister and ring-bearer nephew while holding the ball of yarn. Surely he was explaining the ceremony to them. We established it with the Officiant, Jen, weeks before. Ring-bearer Jaxon would walk with the rings and the yarn down the center as the bridal party entered. Then, at some point, he would travel to the back corner of the guests to start off the string.

I didn't know it at the time, but here's the detail Derek didn't clarify in his instructions; the ball of yarn itself is supposed to stay in the back with the guests, while the rings travel with the *front* end of the string.

If you don't know how yarn works, the yarn is wrapped so that when you start unraveling from the inside the yarn stays steady. If you start from the outside string, the rest of the ball kind of flops around. And flop it did.

Nobody told poor Jaxon this rule about yarn. Jaxon, just 10 at the time, was probably cursing his new aunt for her ridiculously complex ring-bearing operation. To be fair, a pillow and a straight walk down the aisle would have been SO much easier.

The music began, and the grand entrance started. The bridal party made their way down the aisle. My dad walked me down the aisle. All was beautiful, and Derek's eyes welled up when he saw me. I was far too focused on the eyes of the crowd to feel any emotion other than *anxiety*.

I was relieved to join up with Derek at the end of the walk. He was always the steady calm to my nerves.

The time came around for Jaxon to hand the spool to the guest in the back while our officiant explained the ring warming from the altar. Our back guest looped the rings onto the string, and...you guessed it. The guest simply handed the rest of the skein to the person next to them. Instead of a string flowing through the guests, the whole spool went for a *floppy ride*.

My face reddened from the altar as I noticed a floppy purple blob making its way across the guests. I wished I could tell Derek they had it backward, but there was nothing to be done. Jen was already talking.

"When I marry couples, I have them fill out a survey of how they met and some important things they share with each other," the Officiant began, "Welcome guests, I'm honored to be here on this day to celebrate with all of you the marriage of Rhonwyn and Derek..."

I scanned the guests to see where the yarn ball had flopped off to. I noticed Danielle's dad, dressed in his IT-business-casual was holding the ball in his hand. Meanwhile, my glamorous coworker Rachel held her phone out for a photo of her perfectly manicured hand holding onto the rings. Rachel was no doubt giving "good vibes" in the process.

A social media influencer, she would be posting to her Insta stories before we got to the kiss. Guaranteed. The thought of these two guests converging on this ring-warming made me smirk.

My attention was brought back to the altar as Jen instructed us to hold hands and look into each other's eyes.

I nodded my head to the right towards the guests, hoping Derek would somehow read my thoughts. He smiled and breathed deeply–no doubt thinking I needed reassurance.

Jen continued...

"And these are the hands that even when wrinkled and aged will still be reaching for yours, still giving you the same unspoken tenderness with just a touch. May you keep your hands tender as you explore your everlasting and wondrous love."

My attention fell back to the *flopping blob* in the crowd. Uncle Jack and Aunt Glendoris of New Town, "Missourah" prayed deeply on our rings. Imagine their shock if they found out the man holding onto the yarn flop was Iain's boyfriend Kyle; an out-and-proud *gay furry*.

Our string linked the rings through the guests, but it was the tandem ring blessing that truly brought people together in ways that my anxious personality could never imagine.

The time came when the rings got through our wedding party and eventually us, and there was an inherent problem - the rings were in the center of this partially unraveled yarn. We'd have to work our way back up (undoing the blessings?) Or somehow cut the flop off.

From behind me, I heard Jaxon proudly announce "I have a pocket knife."

I turned to take him up on the offer (how lovely would it be for the ring bearer to save the day when there was an issue with the rings?) But he was too slow.

Liam took action, in the process nearly taking out Abie, who, at 5'1" was just about the perfect height of Liam's incoming elbow. Fortunately, a quick dodge kept Abie from any bloodshed.

With the rings now secured, Jen held the microphone to Derek.

"Derek, if you would repeat after me..." It was time. He repeated back each line of vows that we selected weeks prior. It was getting real.

I, Derek, promise to be your lover, companion, and friend,
Your partner in life,
Your ally in conflict,
Your greatest fan and your honest critic,
Your comrade in adventure,
Your student and your teacher.

"Rhonwyn, if you would repeat after me. I Rhonwyn..."

"I Rhonwyn..."

The ceremony continued on, and before we knew it, we were married!

* * *

A lot more went wrong between the wedding and reception, as happens at every wedding, but we somehow managed to make our way to the reception hall in a historic hotel in downtown Flagstaff.

The cake was centered under the window of the other room. It was gorgeous. A three-tiered almond cake with a thin layer of white icing–just enough to see some cake sticking through. When I ordered it months before, I explained to our baker on the phone that I liked naked cakes, but that I liked them "a bit more-than-naked. Like if your cake here is naked" I pointed to one of the cakes on her portfolio for reference, "I'd want a lingerie amount of icing.' She did a great job. Provocative amount of sponge showing, but the cake was no slut.

Then there was the decor. On top of the cake was the cake topper that I'd made myself. Rustic wooden figurines of the pair of us, dressed to match our wedding attire.

Finally, I noticed something unexpected sitting at the foot of the cake. Two things really.

One was the ball of yarn. It was the piece that hadn't been unraveled by the guests. The bit they were flopping throughout the ceremony. It was still perfectly machine-spooled and coiled.

The second was a great mess of yarn wrapped tightly but haphazardly around a 10" stick. Shards of bark that had fallen off the stick during the spooling process stuck like glitter to the yarn.

I wondered which pairing of guests teamed up to make that decision. It was perfect.

* * *

Today, I think of those two spools of yarn at the foot of our wedding cake as an illustration of what the years that followed have been. Sometimes our luck was perfectly machine-pressed. Things just fit perfectly and worked out. Other times, the luck seemed like we were spooled around some old stick getting bark shards all over us from every direction.

But one thing is for sure—the yarn is constant, the love is there, and together, we can take on whatever life decides to deal us.

A Roast for the Happy Couples

There comes a time in every twenty-something's life when the wedding invitations start rolling in. Derek puts on a tie, and I try to fight some volume into my relentlessly straight hair. We watch the bride and groom exchange vows, Derek and I hold hands, and then, at the reception, we have a little tradition that keeps the spark alive in our marriage: we judge the couple.

I'm talking no-holds-barred. You better believe that if I've been to your wedding, I've bet on the longevity of your marriage. (You're so welcome for the card.)

So, without further ado, I give you a definitive ranking of our friends' weddings, cakes, and ultimately, marriages. **In cake order, of course; worst to best:**

STEPHEN AND AMY

Wedding Style:

Morning Church Wedding

Cake:

0 Stars. Donuts guys, really?

Pros:

Derek and I were brand new to Ohio when we attended Derek's colleague, Stephen's *dry* morning wedding (see cons). The reception was over by 2 PM, so we spontaneously invited a few other colleague guests to our house afterward (where there was alcohol). This was a great chance to bond and get to know our new Ohio friends.

1. The bride, Amy, seemed to have hired supermodels as friends to gorgeously sachet down the aisle to Dario Marianelli's version of Purcell's *Dido And Aeneas*. The one from the Kiera Knightley *Pride and Prejudice* Movie. It was just so intense and beautiful. I tear up every time I hear that song. Beautiful choice. If you're reading this and don't know it, go listen to it and come back to the book, I'll wait.

2. Stephen was doing his dissertation on fish locomotion, so the couple had live fishbowls on every table. I was slightly concerned for the welfare of the fish when it came time to close out the nuptials, but Stephen and Amy are not those kinds of people, so these fish had a future arranged for them in a pond at their boss's house. Get this–the fish are thriving there to *this very day*. Generations of baby fish have been born because of this wedding. And this is the first of two examples of how Stephen and Amy proved us wrong (see prognosis).

Rhonwyn's Cons:

1. This couple had a morning wedding *(we're talking 9:00 AM) and* a dry wedding (we're talking nothing; not even champagne to toast the couple.). Stephen/Amy - if you're reading this. I tried to spin that as a pro for you guys, but I had to meet Derek's colleagues completely sober. Unforgivable. This goes into cons.

2. We were entertained by Musician Stephen serenading Amy with a song he wrote on his guitar. He wasn't bad. Actually, it was a sweet song. But this sort of thing is cute at rom-coms or when you have liquor in you, but I remind you, this was a DRY wedding. I can't stress this enough. DON'T google Stephen's song. Google *Dido And Aeneas* again.

3. No cake. The couple wanted to share with their friends and family their love for a local sub-par doughnut shop. They had every doughnut you can imagine, all in shades of blue and purple to blend effortlessly in with the decor. Donut people were happy I guess. I say go cake or go home.

Derek's Cons*:

1. "What? You want me to judge Stephen & Amy's wedding? No."

Prognosis:

Too young. 96% chance of a certain divorce within one year of marriage.

Results:

Wrong! 5 years and a menagerie of fur- and scale-babies.

MARIAH AND DAVID

Wedding Style:

Hastily-Planned Military Wedding for Benefits

Cake:

[File not Found] I don't remember. Can you believe it; me, not remembering a cake? It automatically takes second place because it's better than donuts. But honest to God, don't remember.

Pros:

1. This was the first wedding we attended as a couple, way back in 2015! Derek and I had been dating for about 6 months at the time I got invited to Mariah and Dave's wedding. I asked if Derek would be my plus 1. We held hands awkwardly as we listened to the wedding vow exchange. We also watched Dave's first view of his bride, which is always my favorite part of a wedding. We had no idea if our relationship was going anywhere, but those butterflies were fluttering through the ceremony.

2. Mariah and I had kept in touch on social media since

rooming together in college, but that was it. It had been a solid 5 years since I'd seen her last before the wedding, and a lovely reunion! You only really see the bride for 4 minutes at the wedding, but it was a great time. And receiving one of her over-the-top hugs took me back to our college days.

3.   This was the first wedding I attended that included an afterparty! Like even after the reception, guests would meet up at a bar. This was mostly the younger guests (though I was impressed by some of her night owl aunts and uncles). Since this party was much smaller, I got to chat more with the bride and buy her a drink.

Rhonwyn's Cons:

1.   Remember that after-party? This was the wedding that I learned that Derek is an 85-year-old man who needs to be in bed by 10 PM at the latest. I went solo to the after-party as my new boyfriend snoozed peacefully in the hotel. Not knowing that this was just how he operates, I was a bit disappointed that he didn't want to spend time getting to know my friend. Especially one I hadn't seen in years.

2.   This was the last time I saw Mariah. There was never a fight or falling out, just time and distance drifted us apart. I sent an invite to my wedding years later to her dad's old address, naively hoping that she might show up. Unlike relationships, the hard part about friendships ending is you never get the same closure.

Derek's Cons*:

1.   "Well, results speak for themselves on that one."

Prognosis:

Eight years max. Military culture + Mariah's general love of kids: this marriage is going down in flames and traumatizing kids in the process. Custody battles, whole nine yards.

Results:

No kids, but otherwise...I'm just saying, the prognosis was close. *Is it the judging? Is that why she doesn't talk to me?*

CHRIS AND HILLARY

Wedding Style:

Party Catholics

Cake:

3.5 Stars. Standard almond cake with white icing. The trend of naked cakes was dying by the time Chris and Hillary's wedding rolled around. It was replaced with the slightly-clothed simplistic cake. Chris and Hillary's cake had a splash of glitter on the icing for fun. It was a gorgeous cake, but fell to the fault of what the Great British Baking Show would call "style over substance." The flavor just wasn't anything to write home about.

Pros:

1. I had just started my new job at Ohio Broadway Play-house in Cleveland (OBPHiC) about 6 months prior when I found out there were not one but TWO weddings in the marketing department. I was excited that Chris invited me to his wedding to Hillary. Their wedding was just two weeks be-fore Bethany's Wedding to Kyle (See below). I'd always kept work and personal life separate, but Chris and Hillary's wed-ding was when my coworkers started to become my friends. Arguably graying the lines of a work/life balance, (but more on that later.)

2. Bubbles as the newlyweds left the church! What a cute addition. Hillary is a fashion designer, which doesn't quite align with wedding planning, but you could tell her eye for design appeared in her decor. The bubbles would make a beautiful picture of the happy couple leaving the church.

Rhonwyn's Cons:

1. This was hardly the couple's fault, but OBPHIC was an-nouncing three shows that weekend. The contracts weren't signed until Friday Night, so I was told that evening that emails to buyers had to be out by 10:00 AM. I spent the morning of Chris's wedding trying to curl my hair while pulling a list to send an announcement email to audiences to buy their tickets. Unfortunately, there were issues with my VPN, so I had to call the IT guys. It was a mess. Of course, better than Chris on that day, but it still wasn't a great start to

a wedding. (Chris - if you're reading this, I'm not deducting points on this one. Not your fault!)

2.   Chris and Hillary's morning church wedding was scheduled for about 11 AM, but the reception didn't start until 4. As guests, we had about four hours to kill while the couple got their professional wedding photos taken around Cleveland. Being about an hour from home, Derek and I joined my coworkers and several other party guests in visiting the nearby Summit Mall while we waited for the reception. The wedding guests were all dressed in our wedding attire wandering around Dick's Sporting Goods and Claire's for the better part of the afternoon.

3.   Having marked one full year of marriage by the time of this wedding, Derek and I were excited for the Marriage Length dance game. You know the one. Traditionally, the DJ will play music, and gradually kick couples off the dance floor if they've been married for less than a certain amount of time. I was so excited that our milestone meant we could keep dancing for an extra 30 seconds or so. A couple seated with us at the OBPHiC table had just celebrated their 10 years, they were expecting to hit a solid minute of dancing, or more. But what does this DJ do? He kicks everyone married less than fifteen years within the first 10 seconds! Utter obliteration. The dance floor broke in half like it was hit by Thanos's snap. We all returned to the table in shame.

Derek's Cons*:

1.   "Aren't you friends with Chris? And Hillary seemed nice. Plus I considered the mall adventure a pro."

Prognosis:

This one was hard, we didn't really know them well at the time. The one thing that seemed to go against them was the four-hour wait while they took pictures. Maybe this wedding was just all for the 'gram? 15 years.

Results:

5 years married with a little one on the way!

BETHANY AND KYLE

Wedding Style:

Full Catholic Mass

Cake:

4.5 Stars. Bethany wasn't an influencer back then, but after her wedding, she would grow about 6 thousand followers on her Instagram travel account. This should give you an idea of the type of cake Bethany would have. Her reception was in an immaculate lake house that they decorated with thousands, I mean THOUSANDS of flowers. Her cake pulled off the balance of rustic yet timeless charm. She even had a wooden cake topper that included the Bride, Groom, and their puppy. (How sweet is that?)

The flavor was there to back it up. She had two options; Derek got chocolate and I got white cake. Both were baked to absolute perfection. It's so hard for me not to put Bethany and Kyle's cake in first place, but their fillings were average at best. Close second... Very close.

Pros:

1. Since it was a historic building, there was a cast-iron bench in the shower of the women's restroom, and apparently a bathtub in the men's bathroom. Just coming off the high of Nick's wedding two weeks prior, our work group had fun taking pictures and enjoying the behind-the-scenes of the otherwise immaculate reception hall.

2. Prom Picture! My maroon-purple dress matched her fall color palette. Everyone at our table took turns taking photos of couples in front of the fireplace backdrop, and Derek and I got a gorgeous photo of ourselves that I like to put in my seasonal frame every fall!

3. Bethany and Kyle let us take home gorgeous mums that lasted all season! I told you we were talking THOUSANDS of flowers. I'm glad I got a souvenir.

Rhonwyn's Cons:

1. Full. Catholic. Mass. This could actually be seen as a pro as well. Derek had never attended a Catholic Mass (wedding or otherwise). The priest began... "*Ave Maria gratia plena. Dominus tecum. Benedicta tu in mulieribus...*" Derek's eyes widened--they looked like they were going to pop out of his skull! I tried SO hard to stifle my laugh. Then came the part when the congregation replies "Amen." Another shock for Derek. I snorted 3 or four times *during prayer* trying to keep my laugh contained. *Humiliating.* The lie I told Bethany

later (in case anyone reported my laughing to her) was that one of Kyle's friends was hovering on the balcony, and I thought he was a statue until he moved. She totally bought it. Until she reads this. (*Hi, Beth! Sorry for laughing during prayer at your wedding.*)

2.   This is hardly their fault, but because we had just had a marketing department wedding for Chris two weeks prior, we were all slightly less enthusiastic about the second wedding. With the newlywed guests in attendance for Bethany's wedding, we tried to catch them up on the inside jokes from the last one. It just is never the same.

Derek's Cons*:

1.   "Wait, let me look at this ... You're diagnosing everyone's marriages too? Oh my God. You're the worst."

Prognosis:

Full Catholic Mass always yields a forever marriage. Who knows if they'll be happy behind closed doors, but even if they hate each other, they'll be married for life.

Results:

Still going strong. (From what we can tell...)

KELSEY AND JOHN

Wedding Style:

Outdoor Barn Wedding

Cake:

Five stars. Chef's Kiss. I can't go into details because this cake was so good that it's listed as a pro below.

Pros:

1.   Kelsey was a middle school friend I reconnected with during my Missouri years. She had no intention of inviting me until our reconnection 2-3 months before her wedding. We went on a double date with Kelsey and her fiance and hit it off as couple friends instantly. John and Derek talked about video games, and Kelsey and I gossiped about where our old middle school classmates ended up. We even found out we had similar love stories. Kelsey and John dated briefly in college before breaking up, seriously dated and/or entered failed marriages with others, then reconnected in a fairy-tale rom-com kind of way.

2.   They had board games at their wedding reception. Our table had Clue, and we were positioned with John's work friends who were super into the board game scene. I dominated at Clue. My strategy is intentionally guessing the murderer to be someone in my hand, thus forcing another player to tell me something about the murder weapon, and

so on. Derek eventually caught on to this and was shocked and appalled at my strategy. It was a great time.

3. The cake! (see above) Kelsey and John got married 3 months before Derek and I did. I hadn't given much thought to my wedding cake. Planning an out-of-state wedding, the cake just wasn't a big deal to me. But once I tasted Kelsey and John's orange-raspberry perfection, I had major FOMO. Kelsey told me she hated her cake at her first failed marriage, so this one was a big deal. Good tip. Too late.

Rhonwyn's Cons:

1. **Alyssa Czerenko-Greer.** My middle school nemesis. The girl who made the 7th-grade living hell for me then added salt in the wound 10 years later by taking a penny from the TIP jar at Starbucks where I was working. Yep, she was there. Married now. Apparently, Kelsey and Alyssa got to know each other more after high school. No, I did not say hi.

Derek's Cons*:

1. "You know we're never going to be invited to a wedding again if you publish these, right?"
2. "Oh wait, Kelsey and John's wedding? My con is Clue. That you're a liar. That I learned my wife will employ any means necessary to win a board game. Including lying to the love of her life."

Prognosis:

Kelsey and John have to make it. Their love story mirrors ours so well. They even had a kid about a year before our kid! If ever

> they break up, Derek and I will break up 3 months later. They're our future. So I hope it's a lifetime thing.
>
> Results:
>
> DIVORCED...
> ... Just kidding. Going on 7 years of marriage now. And with a sweet little 5-year-old kiddo!

We have 3 weddings to attend in the next year. Who's ready for *CAKE 2*?

Step 4

Bake at 350°

Meeting David Sedaris

"Happy No-Sex Date!" Derek was far too enthusiastic for this sentiment–what a change trying to conceive a child can have on a guy.

Derek opened the passenger door for me, and I gave him a quick peck on the lips as I got out.

It was October 30th. This meant we had *officially* been trying to get pregnant for a year and a month.

Two months of casually not-trying-not-preventing turned into five months of calendar trying. This then turned into four more months of calendar-trying while I googled "when to see a fertility specialist" from the bed for 15 minutes while my butt was propped up on a pillow to help gravity encourage sperm to move downward closer to the egg. This was all followed by two months of the decision to "just have sex every other day," while I prayed to a god I didn't believe in that this would be the month.

We knew I had PCOS, meaning I wasn't ovulating every month. There was a reason, but the trying was getting me down. Why did it have to be *this* of all things that I was bad at?

After my September pregnancy test came back negative, we agreed it was time to start talking about a fertility doctor. Ever the calm one, Derek suggested that before we do all that, we take it easy for a few weeks and just relax. His suggestion was that we could just have some "not-trying-not-preventing," fun throughout the holiday season and maybe pick it up again in January.

The year 2020 seemed so far in the future, my eyes watered up at the thought of it.

Derek pulled me in for a hug, and kissed the top of my head–it didn't take any words for him to know what I was thinking. It was one of his best qualities.

"How's this," he suggested, "If January's too far, then why don't we just wait on the fertility thing until after the David Sedaris show?"

My coworker Natalie had scored us box tickets to see David Sedaris live at *Ohio Broadway Playhouse in Cleveland*. David does Cleveland every other year, and he performed the day I interviewed at OBPHiC two years prior, so I missed my chance by a thread in 2017. I was very much looking forward to this show.

"We'll have a whole date night." Derek added, "You can have a drink, which you haven't really done since we started trying. Just have a relaxing fun evening, then worry about planning afterward. We won't even have sex. The spirit is willing, but the flesh is spongy and bruised" Derek assured me, quoting Futurama.

We had a deal. Fertility specialist in November, but first, the "No-Sex Date." We would take it easy.

We settled into our seats at *Cibreo*, the fancy Italian restaurant across from OBPHiC. Normally, if we were going to a show at work, we'd go somewhere like Yours Truly. We're pretty frugal, but this was a *date*, so we were going to treat ourselves.

I ordered a glass of red wine with dinner. And a second with dessert.

The buzz hit me quick! I had given up alcohol almost immediately after starting to try to conceive. I'd heard it contributed to issues conceiving. Plus, I figured if I were to get pregnant, I wouldn't want to be drinking anyway. This was certainly a break.

"I feel bad that you're not getting anything special to treat yourself," I told Derek. I was slightly exaggerating my slurred speech because it seemed fun to be drunk. He was never much of a wine drinker.

"I might get dessert." He said, face into the menu. "Oooh, Tiramisu!"

"You can't have Tiramisu here," I told him, my voice carrying further than anticipated.

"Why not?"

"You know what happens when you eat tiramisu."

"What do you mean?"

"Every time you eat tiramisu, you forget there's cocoa powder on top, so you breathe it in and then cough all over. It's gross. This place is fancy."

"You're drunk," he said, insinuating I don't know my own husband's reaction to cakes.

"Nooooo." I exaggerated into my glass.

Derek and I split a to-*die*-for tiramisu. Some people get it wrong, putting too much vanilla into the batter to compensate for the coffee. But Tiramisu needs to be a bit bitter, a bit coffee, a perfect combination of sponge ladyfingers and chocolate coffee decadence.

Sure enough, with the first bite, he stifled two coughs. But I'll admit, he managed to do it without opening his mouth.

"Told you," I said, letting him take more than half of the dessert.

I swallowed the rest of my wine, feeling my cheeks warm up from the booze. Derek polished off every last crumb of Tiramisu.

"This is fun," I told my husband.

"I'm glad," he said.

With dinner and dessert, it was time for the show. We paid the server quickly and rushed across the street next to OBPHiC's famous Lamp Post; it's World-famous for claiming the title of Northeastern Ohio's Largest Outdoor Lamp Post made of Iron... So they say anyway.

* * *

When the show was over, I took my place in line to get my book signed by David Sedaris! The line wrapped all the way from the MuniBank Ohio Theater Lobby, up the steps to the balcony entrance, around the upper bar, and back down the steps on the other side. I looked at my phone: 10:45. It was going to be a late night.

"I'm gonna go do a raid," Derek told me, taking out his phone for Pokémon.

"Nerd," I said.

"Says the person about to stand in line for two hours to get a book signed." Derek kissed me, "I might also nap somewhere. That bench looks comfy. I'm tired."

I flipped through my copy *of Holidays on Ice*. I had a habit of pushing David Sedaris's books on everyone I met. Unfortunately, *Me Talk Pretty One Day*--my favorite of his collection--was still at Natalie's house ... (*Actually, she still has it. I'm going to have to ask her about that when I'm done writing this...*)

The girl in front of me in the book signing line had four books. While chatting in line, she explained to me that she heard David was a multiple-book signer, so she'd try her luck. I thought that was kind of rude. I was more into the prospect of a conversation with him than I was into making him sign four books. But then again, I was never much of an autograph collector, so what did I know?

Hours passed as I made the way up the stairs, across the balcony, and back down the side. Derek came and went, doing God knows what in between. I finally got to the table at 2:15AM.

I was surprised by how nervous I was when I saw him. He seemed like a normal enough guy. Bald head, aging around his eyes. He'd have to have been in his sixties by that point.

"Hello!" He said with a toothy grin that I recognized from his About the Author pages. "Let's see…" He looked at the slip of paper we were instructed to fill out with the spelling of our names.

"Rhonwyn? Is that Welsh?"

Of course, he knew it was Welsh. He's brilliant, and he'd lived in France for a few years, so he's bound to have explored Europe a bit.

"Yep! Welsh," I confirmed

Behind the table, Natalie was sorting some paperwork with David's staff. She heard my voice and let David know "This is my coworker I was telling you about!"

"Oh!" David said, straightening up taller in his seat. I smiled knowing that Natalie's opinion mattered so much to him.

"How old are you, Rhonwyn?"

I felt embarrassed to answer, I must have looked exceedingly young to him with my hair pulled into a braid.

"Twenty-eight," I told him. I felt like even more of a child answering questions without elaboration. *Am I starstruck?* I wondered.

"Oh really, 28?" he said, "Do you have *a baby?*"

At first, I didn't think about my struggle of the past year. In fact, quite the opposite. I felt more like my 16-year-old self lying to the family doctor and *insisting* that I'm not sexually active. Far, far too young to have any kind of kid.

"Oh God, no, none of that yet." I heard myself assure him.

I questioned my tone instantly after. *Why did I answer like that?* I thought, drifting away from the conversation in front of me. I had been trying to conceive for over a year! I was looking into fertility options.

"Sorry, I don't know why I asked that. I don't think you're supposed to ask people that." David Sedaris said, in an almost awkward tone.

David doodled some Christmas trees into my book.

I walked away from the table, even more disappointed by the inter-action. *How fun would it have been if I was pregnant?* I imagined, how *fun would it have been to announce a pregnancy that way... "No, David Sedaris, I don't have a baby, but I'm pregnant!"*

He could sign something like, "Welcome Rhonwyn's baby ❤" into my book instead of his doodles of vaguely phallic Christmas trees. (or both!) But alas, I wasn't pregnant. And my icon had just inadvertently rubbed it in my face that I didn't have a baby.

Derek and I drove home quietly, getting in the door at 3:55AM. I didn't even think Derek knew that there were two 3:55s in a day, but he managed.

True to our word, exhaustion set it and there was no sex that night.

* * *

I slept clear until 11:45 the next morning. I woke up with a hangover and a desperate need to pee.

I grabbed a pregnancy test... *Why not?* I figured. I peed and waited for the obligatory two minutes.

There it was.

A line.
The line. The *second* line.
The line I'd hoped to see test after test after test in that stupid oval. It was faint, but it was a *line*.

"Uh.... Derek?" I said flatly from the bathroom.
"What did I do now?" he called, already playing video games.
I walked to the living room with the test in hand.

"Does this look like a line to you?"

Lay Off The ~~Brakes~~ Cakes

I'd been working for *Ohio Broadway Play House in Cleveland* for about three years when Valentine's Day rolled around again. Ever the theatrical crowd, OBPHiC's very own Joanie Edgeworth, my cube neighbor and perhaps the most famous person I will *ever* meet, organized a Valentine's Day sweets buffet for the staff. This was a spectacle you wouldn't believe! Valentine's Day was planned MONTHS in advance. In fact, the day after Christmas, Joanie would begin baking and freezing brownies, cookies, cakes, and sweets of every kind to feature in the holiday. A signup email went around in early January from Joanie, giving the opportunity for any other employees to contribute. Naturally, I had to sign my name up to share some homemade Gooey Butter Cake with these Ohioans.

Gooey Butter Cake is a cornerstone of the St. Louis food scene. As St. Louis-isms are concerned, Gooey Butter Cake ranks up there with eating Italian food on The Hill, complaining about Imo's Pizza, and asking your 45-year-old neighbor what high school they went to.

This dessert is made up of only five ingredients; yellow cake mix, eggs, vanilla extract, cream cheese, and (you guessed it) butter. The sheer amount of wet ingredients gives the dessert a unique moist brownie-like consistency, but instead of chocolate, the flavor of a rich buttery yellow cake. Optional - top the whole thing with a ton of confectioner's sugar and you too can contract your own type two diabetes (more on that later).

These days you can't mention Gooey Butter Cake in St. Louis without noting that Paula Deen once put forth a recipe called "Ooey Gooey Cake," which she lifted straight from a St. Louis cookbook and claimed for her own. Deen has since been canceled in the state of Missouri, but that's neither here nor there.

"Are you all ready for Valentine's Day, Joanie?" I overheard our CEO, Pru, ask one snowy morning in January. OBPHiC didn't claim to organize the event or sanction any part of it, but they *did* allow her to commandeer a conference room in the name of some holiday cheer.

"Oh yes, Tim is ready for me to take all of my brownies out of our second freezer," said Joanie, entering into a story about Valentine's Day 1998 in which their freezer actually *stopped* working in January and she had to bring the treats into work to store in the break room a few weeks early. Imagine the look on the Security Guard Darrell's face when she caught him sneaking a cupcake! ... and so on.

Pru nodded on as Joanie then continued to remind her of Valentine's Day 2003 when the big winter storm *canceled* Valentine's Day. They had to reschedule for the 16th! Can you believe it? I was only listening in and out of the conversation, but I'm fairly certain I heard that Air Force One got involved.

"Are you making anything, Rhonwyn?" Pru looked to me to include me in the conversation. I daresay Pru was asking for help out of hearing another Valentine's Day story.

"Yes!" I said enthusiastically, "*You'll* be especially happy to know I'm making some *Gooey Butter Cake* this weekend."

Pru grew up in Eureka, Missouri, about an hour out of St. Louis. She'd certainly have moved to Cleveland long before I was even born, but I loved to have a piece of home in common with our CEO.

"Oh I can't wait," said Pru. "I haven't had Gooey Butter Cake in an age. You'll love it, Joanie."

"I'm sure," Joanie said, flashing a wide grin across her perfectly made-up red lips. "Rhonwyn's been telling me she just had to share a piece of St. Louis with the Marketing Team."

"That's so wonderful. How are you feeling by the way?" Pru turned her attention to me, asking about my growing belly.

"I'm alright, thanks!" I told her, "The morning sickness has definitely subsided now that I'm in the second trimester.

* * *

When the holiday finally arrived, I fastened my Gooey Butter Cake carefully in the passenger seat as I made my 1-hour commute up to Cleveland. On top of that was a bright pink Valentine's Day Thank-You card I'd prepped for my cube neighbor. Betty Boop with a heart apron. I thought it was appropriate for the occasion.

There were icy roads that day to be sure, but Clevelanders balked at any snowfall under 12 inches. And let's face it, there was *no* calling out of work on OBPHiC's big staff event.

I maneuvered my car through the ice, pressing the brakes every few miles—less for the snow, but more for the sheer number of cars on the road. It was bumper to bumper. I was relieved to be pregnant enough to have the ability to keep down a warm herbal tea throughout my commute, but not yet *so* pregnant that I'd have to stop to pee. The timing was everything.

Speaking of-- I glanced at the clock. 8:47, and I wasn't at the Plain Dealer Building yet. I'd be late for sure. It was dead-stop traffic, so I took a final chug of my drink and returned it to the cupholder, noticing something moving *quickly* in my rearview mirror.

SHIT - I knew instantly that it was going to hit. All I could do was minimize the impact. I let off the brakes and winced in anticipation, curling my toes tight.

SLAM!

Everything lurched forward as our cars collided. Out of the corner of my eye, I saw Joanie's bright red card fall straight onto the floor in front of the passenger seat.

I stepped on the brakes again to stop myself from hitting the car in front of me.

Then, just as quickly, everything was still again.

I exhaled in relief. *It's just a fender bender,* I told myself.

I looked in the rearview mirror to see if the other driver was okay. He was already walking toward me. He looked young, maybe a year or two younger than me. He was dressed in business casual with a school logo on his badge, probably a high school teacher. I rolled down the window, letting in a gust of frigid winter air.

'I'm SO sorry. I gotta be honest... I was checking my email and then I... I just didn't... are you *okay*?!"

I assured him I was alright and that we should probably move over to the side of the road to talk. It was rush hour and this was I70 North, right into Cleveland.

Once we were safely on the shoulder, I wrapped my coat around myself, grateful that my stomach was still flat enough to zip up my jacket. It shielded me from the frigid wind. Making my way over to the back of the car, I rested my hand on my stomach, just below my belly button.

"Hope you're okay in there," I told my belly, trying on a parenting voice as you'd try on a new pair of shoes. It fell flat. It still wasn't real yet.

We exchanged insurance information and phone numbers. I took pictures of both of our cars and texted them to him. It was a trick I'd picked up working at the law firm all those years ago.

The law firm, I thought. *Personal injury--it can be hours before you feel an injury because of the adrenaline.* I turned to the driver, who was shivering in the cold.

"Hey so I have to be honest," I started, "I feel totally fine, but I'm 20 weeks pregnant, so I am going to go run to urgent care or something to get checked out."

"Oh my God, you're PREGNANT?" his eyes nearly welled up with guilt, "I feel even worse. I'm so sorry--"

"I'm okay, I'm sure. Look, if I wasn't pregnant I wouldn't even go to the doctor, this was nothing. Just wanting to be sure baby's alright."

"Yes, of course. Oh my God, of course. I understand. God, keep me posted on the baby, please. I feel so bad."

We stood in the winter wind waiting for a cop to show up to make a police report. I opened my door to sit down in the backseat and send some texts. Ever the workaholic, I texted my boss immediately.

MATT

> Hey, I was just in a car accident. Everyone's okay, but I'm going to go get checked out just in case, so I'll probably be in late.

OMG! Yes, of course, take as long as you need.

Sliding my phone back in my pocket, I turned my attention to the other driver. He was hunched over and sending his own texts to various bosses and loved ones.

"God my mom's so mad I hit a pregnant girl," he confessed to me, red from the howler he'd received.

"It's fine. I'm fine, I promise." I reassured him. "Here, do you want some gooey butter cake? I made it for work for Valentine's day."

"Oh right, it's Valentine's Day! No. I can't–I shouldn't have any cake."

The "shouldn't" in his voice sounded like he was withholding the offer as some kind of atonement.

I tried a few more times, but the poor kid was not going to be eating any Gooey Butter cake that morning.

Still waiting on the cop to arrive, I went back to my car. The wind was relentless, and my eyes were tearing up from the blistering cold. I quickly realized I hadn't texted Derek yet! His pregnant wife was just in a crash and he had no idea. Whoops.

I opened my phone to my text chain with Matt so I could copy and paste.

DEREK

Hey, I was just in a car accident. Everyone's okay, but I'm going to go get checked out just in case. Love you. ❤

Okay. I love you. Do you want me to meet you anywhere?

No, it's really just a fender bender. All is fine, I'm sure.

I called my OBGYN. No luck. Apparently they were closed on Tuesdays. The after-hours service instructed me to go to the ER instead of Urgent Care since the hospital would have Imaging. Great, I thought, a 4-hour wait at ER. I guess I can work from my phone.

MATT

Hey, so I think I'm just going
to take the whole day off, actually.
It'll be a long wait.

Of course. Keep us posted!

Finally, the blue and red lights made their way past the gridlock of traffic.

With the report complete, I turned the car back to I70 South and made the long trek back to my hospital. I was less angry about the car accident but more angry about the fact that it happened 3 miles from work. Couldn't it have been right after I left? 45 minutes to Cleveland, 40 minutes on the side of the highway, and 45 minutes back to the Cuyahoga Falls Hospital. This was basically a road trip to nowhere. At least I could snack on Gooey Butter Cake from the passenger seat. (It was wasted otherwise, and without food, I'd start feeling nauseous.

* * *

It was approaching 10:30 by the time I finally got to the Emergency Department. They whisked me away. I was startled by how quickly they gave me a room.

My anxiety shot up. *They only give real emergencies this kind of attention.* I thought to myself. Years prior, when Derek met my family for the first time, Derek's pinky finger got smashed with a medicine ball that my dad threw at him. He and my dad sat in the ER for *SIX HOURS* watching more damaged ER guests skip right past triage before Derek could even be seen. But here I was, pregnant and in a car accident, skipping triage. *Should I have not waited for the police report?*

I didn't have much time to worry before they brought a wheelchair to my room to bring me back for imaging.

Marleen from Imaging squirted warm gel on my stomach. This was my second ultrasound. Our first was to find out the gender, but Derek and I wanted to wait before we found out. We had planned to do a light gender reveal at our baby shower in April. Not the whole point of the party, but a fun activity to find out with the family and friends. So when we had our OB appointment, we asked them to put the gender-related sonograms in an envelope for us. I glanced at my purse, which was slumped over on a seat. The envelope was still inside. It held so much hope. I worried more about my little one. Boy or girl didn't matter.

"Ah, here we go! A healthy strong heartbeat. See that thump on the screen right there?"

I breathed a sigh of relief. There was my baby. Their little spinal cord bumps were up against the front of the screen. Behind it was a rapid white flash that I'd come to recognize as a heartbeat.

"I'm just going to record a few other vitals." she reassured me, "Standard precaution, but everything's looking really good."

The baby moved as Marleen moved the scanner across my stomach, trying unsuccessfully to get a good photo of Baby's brain and organs.

"You've got an active little guy in there!" Marleen said with a smile.

"They did that last scan too–it was a new game!"

I watched as Marleen moved the scanner to reveal a big head and tiny feet. Then I caught a good glimpse of baby butt. And I was no professional, but between those little butt cheeks was what looked to me like a textbook penis. *A boy.*

I smiled, deciding at that moment to keep this little mommy-son secret from Derek. He would find out in April.

They wheeled me back to my ER room. I had four missed emails. Chris's was marked "important."

> From: Chris Milton
> Subject: FWD: Show Cancelled DO NOT ANNOUNCE
>
> Hey Rhonwyn,
>   That 70's Musical Tour that was supposed to be announced today is wanting to cancel. They need their artwork changed ASAP and the email to not go out.

Shit. That 70's Musical was managed by our neediest tour company. I'd hear about it if any info got up on the site. Plus the email was scheduled to auto-send to all 60,000 newsletter subscribers at Noon, and it was already 11:46.

> From: Rhonwyn Crownover
> Subject: RE: FWD: Show Cancelled DO NOT ANNOUNCE
>
> Hi Chris,
>   So I was in a car accident today, so I'm not going in. I'm not even near a computer to cancel it. Can you ask Matt?

Not wanting to risk waiting for a response, I texted Matt myself.

MATT

> Did you see Chris's email? We need to cancel That 70's Musical Announcement but I'm still at the ER. Everything seems fine. Email scheduled at 10 AM. It's in the BWAY-2020 Folder.

Yes... Actually, can I call real quick? Seriously, tell me no if you have to go.

Before I could reply, there was a knock at the door. It was a doctor this time, holding a clipboard. Hopefully, that meant all was well.

"Good news." Said the doctor, reviewing his notes, "Everything seems absolutely normal. Both you and the baby seem healthy. We're going to have to keep you until the on-call pediatrician has the final sign-off, since you're over 20 weeks. He's reviewing his notes now. Just a protocol. But you can get dressed and pack up."

Wow, I thought. It was shocked that a pediatrician had to review anything. Twenty weeks would be extremely, premature, but the fact that they had to sign off meant Baby was viable at that point. It sunk in that I was going to be a mom in just a few short months.

"That's great, thank you so much." I told him.

"Unrelated to the crash though," The doctor continued, "There were some small traces of sugar in your urine. You're not diabetic normally, are you? I didn't see it on your chart."

"No, not diabetic."

"Okay well, it could be a sign of gestational diabetes. Might want to get that checked out. Though at 20 weeks, you probably have that scheduled here soon anyway."

"Oh yeah, actually I go in for labs next week." I told him.

"Great, well, I'll leave a note here just for your OB."

"Thanks."

I left the hospital with my paperwork and a few bonus sonograms in hand. With the other, I cradled my belly. I hadn't really done that up until that day. I'd always thought of it as kind of performative when I saw other pregnant women do it. But that day felt different. I knew my little *boy* was in there, and that he was safe.

"Hear that Jasper," I said, balancing my way across the icy parking lot. The parenting voice came naturally this time. "Doctor says we have to take it easy on the cake."

Sheet Cake & Grippy Socks

June 25.

Jasper Jurestovsky was born on June 25, 2020. His face was squished and bruised from birth. He had strawberry lines down the front of his nose and a freckle just above his right eyebrow. I couldn't help but stroke his cheek. It was softer than silk, and he seemed to be soothed by it enough. As the cries stopped, he looked at me as if to let me know that I belonged to him.

"Hi Jasper," I introduced myself, "I'm your Mama."

Jasper started to coo, and I was consumed by *responsibility*. I was holding this baby that I'd dreamed of for years, and not only did I have to protect him and help him grow, but I also had to do it in the middle of a pandemic. (Middle, ha! It was just starting.) My spine shivered. *Am I qualified to do this?*

June 28.

I came back home from the hospital with my new sleeping baby in tow. I placed his car seat carrier in the center of the living room and took in my odd surroundings. My makeshift pandemic office setup still intruded on the living room. Having reassigned the old office to a nursery, we were forced to make due in March when everyone was sent home to work in quarantine. The wooden chair I'd sat on for the past 3 months was tucked into the entry table turned desk.

I jiggled the mouse out of curiosity. The glow of my laptop returned OBPHiC's marketing automation platform, frozen in time. Just the way I left it. Just days ago, I had been busy sending out messages about our company's commitment to return to the stage by Fall of 2020. Now, I wondered if my colleagues would reunite and make progress before I even returned from my maternity leave. I hoped they wouldn't.

I felt a pang of unease. I had been so laser-focused on nesting through this COVID-19 pandemic, I'd neglected to fully nest for a baby. I had been so sure this COVID-19 thing would pass by the time the little guy came. I was wrong.

My phone buzzed.

NATALIE

OMG, the pandemic got SO MUCH WORSE since you guys went into the hospital. There's
like PLEXIGLASS on all the registers.

Look at These links:
CNN: SARS-COVID-2 Death Toll: A Bleak Milestone Reached in Global Pandemic. Read More. >
Channel 4 News: Summit County Ohio: 933 New Cases As of June 27. Read More. >
HuffPo: Children more likely to DIE of COVID than Elderly: New studies have found. Read More. >
Forbes: Toilet Paper Shortage Contributing to Stock Market Crash Tune in for live updates. >

I returned the phone to my pocket. *I need some air,* I thought, not having the energy to reply to Natalie.

I glanced at Jasper, who was still snoozing in his carrier. Virginia was sniffing his feet. She was unsure about this new smell invading her home.

"You got buddy?" I asked Derek, who was holding his phone up to video the duo.

"Yeah, of course," he said softly.

I stepped onto the porch, taking in the warm fresh air. It was a small relief to soak up the sun again after days in the frigid hospital air conditioning.

From my porch, I noticed trash bags strewn in front of Old Man Jiggs' house across the street. There had to be dozens of them.

"Congratulations! He's beautiful" our other neighbors said from their porch. "We saw you guys walk in earlier."

"Thanks! What's with the trash bags?" I asked, gesturing at Jiggs's house.

"You literally just missed the coroner, they had to take Jiggs's body away about an hour before you guys got home. And the moving van came to move his caregiver out immediately. COVID, I'm sure."

"Oh..." I said. My stomach lurched. *Bring Out Yer Dead.* I couldn't help but picture Rotor from my time as a summer camp counselor.

My head reeled with worry. *I need to check on Jasper. He's been in his carrier for almost an hour. Babies can stop breathing if you leave them inclined for too long. ABC: Alone, on your Back, in a Crib. I need to get him out of there and move him to a crib.*

I waved my neighbor goodbye and scurried back inside.

June 30.

I hadn't slept since leaving the hospital. No, not the newborn-parent no-sleep. Not a wink. Adrenaline and fear kept me up hours after Derek and Jasper fell asleep.

With the extra time alone from not sleeping, I read more and more about babies online. *I haven't taken nearly enough classes,* I thought. *They were all canceled for COVID.* I kept scrolling on my phone. I read more about COVID online.

The light from my phone seared into my corneas.

"Weh" "Weh" "Waaaaah!" Jasper was ready to eat again.

Since I was already awake, I figured I'd let Derek sleep. Maybe after I got him this time, I'd be able to fall asleep after.

Breastfeed.

Fail to Latch.

Finger Feed.

Diaper Change.

Rock Baby.

Put Baby Down.

Pump.

Store the Milk.

Wash the Bottles.

Lie Down.

    I returned to my bed. "Sleep when the baby sleeps," They say... *Might as well try.* Derek had already fallen back asleep from the wakeup.

    My eyes sprang open. Again. Not from baby. This time from worry. *What if he stops breathing? What If I can't hear him? What if he spits up and chokes on it? Will I hear the gurgling?*

    I tossed and turned another 3 hours.

    "Weh" "Weh" "Waaaaah!" Jasper was ready to eat again. Since I was already awake, I figured I'd let Derek sleep.

Breastfeed.

Fail to Latch.

Finger Feed.

Diaper Change.

Rock Baby.

Put Baby Down.

Pump.

Store the Milk.

Wash the Bottles.

Lie Down.

"Sleep when the baby sleeps," They say...

My eyes sprang open. Again. *What if he stops breathing?* I hadn't slept since the first night at the hospital. *What If I can't hear him? What if he spits up and chokes on it? Will I hear the gurgling? It's been 3 hours since he fell asleep. He'll be waking soon and I haven't slept at all.*

"Weh" "Weh" "Waaaaah!" Jasper was ready to eat again...

July 1.

Breastfeed.

Fail to Latch.

Formula Feed.

Diaper Change.

Rock Bottle Baby.

Put Baby Down.

Pump.

Store the Milk.

Lie Down.

"Sleep when the baby sleeps," They say.

My eyes sprang open. Again. *What if he stops breathing?* I hadn't slept since the first night at the hospital. *What If I can't hear him? What if he spits up and chokes on it? Will I hear the gurgling? It's been 3 hours since he fell asleep. He'll be waking soon and I haven't slept at all.*

"Weh" "Weh" "Waaaaah!" Jasper was ready to eat again.

Breastffeed.

Fail to Latch.

Feed Bottle Bottle Bottle Bottle Bottle Baby.

Diaper   Change.

Rock Bottle Baby.

Put   Baby Down . ;;;;;;;;;;;;;

Pump.

Store the.

Lie Dowwwwwn.

"Sleep when the baby sleeps," They say.

My eyes sprang open. Again. I hadn't slept since the first night at the hospital. *What if *I* stop breathing? What if I've forgotten how to breathe in my sleep? Will Derek hear the gurgling?*

Will Jasper have a mom? I hadn't slept since the first night at the hospital.

July 3.

Formula Feed.

Rock Baby.

Feed Bottle Bottle Bottle Bottle Bottle Baby.

Put Baby   Down.

Lie Down.

*   Derek has Jasssssssssssssssssssssssssssssssssper.*

Mom & Dad are asleep upstairs.

*   Check on   Baby.*

Lie DO))))))wN

*   Check on   Baby.*

Lie Down........ Again.

My eyes sprang open. Again. I hadn't slept since the first night at the hospital. "Sleep when the baby sleeps," They say.

I pulled out my phone.

The record length anyone had ever gone without sleep was Randy Gardner in 1963. Randy was awake for a total of 11 days and 25 minutes. I was on day 6– that's 144 hours– and just delivered a baby. *Can my body handle this long?* I wondered. *I just want an hour.* The thought of sleeping pumped anxiety through me. *Is my heart just going to stop if I stop moving? I need to go to the hospital.*

*I was letting everyone down. I'm pulling everyone's attention away from Jasper. I'm making it harder. They'd be better off without me...If I can't sleep, I just want to **die.***

July 4.

Day 7 without sleep was the fourth of July. I had gone 160 hours straight without a wink. I found myself sitting in an ER padded room on suicide watch. I knew I had to go to the hospital to get sleep, but the padded room was not where I'd expected to end up.

I wiggled my toes together from my hospital bed, scrunching the fabric on my oversized hospital-grade socks.

There would be fireworks that night to keep everyone up, I thought, *Not just me. Jasper's going to be so terrified. And Derek and I aren't even with him. At this rate, Derek won't even be back by the time the fireworks start...*

"Your parents have him. He's okay." Derek reassured me. He always seemed to know what I was worrying. Derek had stayed with me the entire 6 hours in ER Triage, waiting for my COVID test to let me pass through so I could be formally admitted.

Derek moved over to my bed so he could hold me. The red dot from the suicide watch camera glared down at us.

"Only one person on the bed" the intercom chastised us. Derek returned to his stool.

It was another hour before the test came back. Negative for COVID. With that result, a nurse who just came on duty was able to give me an Ativan.

"This will knock you out," he said, "you'll sleep tonight."

I popped the pill in my mouth and swallowed it dry. Adding, "Thank you" afterward.

The nurse handed me a plastic cup of water. "Also, since you're negative, we can officially enter you into the Psych Level. Time to transfer you right now."

"Patients only" he clarified, looking at Derek.

After saying our goodbyes, the metal door closed, separating my husband and me through bulletproof glass. I took one last look at Derek. His eyes were wet and bloodshot.

"Ma'am, please lift your arms up and stand with your feet apart" A man in a cop's uniform boomed from behind me.

I complied.

The cop used a metal wand to check me for obvious weapons.

An older woman in scrubs held tight to a clipboard as I was scanned.

"Alright, you're going to come with me behind the curtain to strip down. Your underwear can stay on, but the bra has to go."

She slid the curtain closed, separating us from the cop.

I was already in the paper gown from the Psych Ward at ER, so there wasn't much left to strip.

"I'm sorry" she added. "It's just for everyone's protection."

"Honestly, I just gave birth in front of like 25 people, so at this point, nothing's a mystery." I said dryly as I handed her my bra. It was damp from my milk.

"Ha! Ain't that the truth? Us moms go through a lot don't we?" she folded my bra carefully and tossed it in a black trash bag. "So was this your first baby?"

"Yes, Jasper. He's a week old."

"Remove your ponytail"

I took my ponytail out, letting my thick hair fall to my shoulders.

"I'll put this in a bag with your bra. You can't have hair accessories here."

She eyed me up and down with a pitying look. "Okay, because of your condition, you'll be able to keep your underwear for the duration of your stay, but I need you to pull it down so I can verify you're not hiding anything."

This time I paused. "Um, like I said, I just gave birth a week ago so…"

"Yes, you have a pad on and you're bleeding," The nurse was very matter-of-fact, "That's okay, I've seen it all."

I heard the cop shift the weight of his feet from the other side of the curtain.

A nurse looking up my vagina for weapons was, in fact, more shameful than 25 medical professionals watching a baby come out of it.

* * *

The Psych floor was far colder than the intake room. There was no furniture save for one table at the end of a long fluorescent hallway. An older man with a long gray beard was sitting at the table playing Solitaire. Through the haze of the Ativan, which started kicking in, this scene looked like it was cut straight out of a horror film. I wondered if I was hallucinating.

I wrapped my hospital robe around myself while I took in the scene in the hallway. The Nurse who'd searched me in the ER supplied me with a tattered fabric robe, but there was no belt to pull it tight. *Can't have us hanging ourselves,* I realized.

In a room off the corner of a hallway, a night tech was sitting at a shakily moving some papers. With the amount he was shaking, he looked like he could have been a patient himself. But then again, so did I, so who was I to judge?

He passed the paperwork to me and said something in a thick South African accent. I couldn't understand what he said. Instead, I read the cover of the files.

PSYCHIATRIC PATIENT INTAKE FORM:

72 HOUR EMERGENCY HOLD

72 hours? I thought. *No one told me about 72 hours. I'm just here to get a diagnosis.*

I scanned the page further. Looking for more mentions of the 72 hours. Why did I have to stay that long?

"I just want to get my sleep figured out." I slurred.

By this point, I was fighting the Ativan, more and more confused and tired. Finally, all I wanted was to fall asleep, and had the drugs to do it, but I had to meet with this shaky male tech. I thought they'd be deciding my treatment for me, not committing me.

He said nothing but stared at me with big, overtly-sympathetic eyes. *He's trained to give people that look,* I hypothesized. He tapped the pen to the paper.

A large woman walked into the room. I realized it was doubling as a laundry room. "Oh, that's just what it says, hon. Most people aren't here that long," she told us, shoving several robes into a washing machine. I wasn't sure if her statement was directed to me or the nurse.

I read the page again. ***72 hours.***

"Night tech said stay might be shorter." I scribbled on the side of the paper next to where the time limit was written. The nurse took the paper back and read my note.

"You may be here longer. That's up to the doctor," he condescended in his shaky accent. "Now let's check on what you'll agree to while you're here."

- Patient will eat three (3) meals per day.
- Patient will sleep four hours each night minimum.
- Patient will partake in all assigned group activities.
- Patient will take any prescribed medicine.
- Patient will meet with the hospital psychiatrist to establish a plan of care.

My anxiety surged again. "How long am I going to be here? I just want to see a doctor about my sleep."

The room was spinning and the Ativan was pulling me down into a forced sleep that I knew I couldn't fight much longer. The pen was in my hand. Didn't initial anything.

Dad's advice from years ago echoed in my head. "Don't sign anything without reading it through. That's how they get you."

I tried to focus on the fuzzy letters on the page.

"Do you not agree to these?" The night nurse asked.

"I just want to read it," I told him. "I don't think I'm supposed to stay this long," I added with as much of an assertive tone as I could muster through my sleepy fog.

"That's okay, but while you're here, will you eat food?" he asked, patronizingly.

"Yes, but..." He gestured to the bullet point about eating, and I signed. I would give him that victory.

"While here will you sleep? Tonight?"

"Maybe?" I explained, "That's why I'm here. I can't agree to sleep *'four hours'* each night because I haven't been sleeping at all. That's why I'm trying to talk to the Psych to begin--"

"Okay, well you will talk to the Psych tomorrow. It's after hours right now. Will you lie in bed tonight? I see they gave you Ativan, so I expect you're feeling quite tired."

We battled through the rest of the agreements. I accepted defeat on all of them. The only one I was eager to sign was the final one -- establishing a plan of care. That's all I wanted. Why did it take all this just to get a plan of care?

I just want to sleep.

July 5.

My eyes sprang open. Jasper's cries were echoing in my ears. He sounded so far away he could be underwater. I felt my clothes, damp and heavy with sweat, pulling me back into reality.

I took in the sights above me. It was a gray room. My bed was situated under a fluorescent light that was still turned off. To my left was a barred and frosted window. *To prevent jumping.*

The memories flooded back. The Night Nurse guided me to my bunk.

Did I sleep? I wondered. *I must have.* My body ached. I felt like I'd been hit by a truck.

Chainsaw snores sounded from the right of me. I remembered it was my roommate. She hadn't moved since I got in. Of course, I had no idea how long I'd slept. It was still night, wee hours of the morning at the latest.

I lifted the covers off of me and got an instant whiff of my sweat. It reeked of panic. My breasts had leaked in the night. *Have I smelled like this all week? Or is it just because I finally got a couple of hours of sleep?*

Okay, I thought, *Priority 1 - Shower. Priority 2 - Find psych.*

Of course, there was no shower in our bunk's bathroom. It made sense in a psychiatric facility. Right off the bat, I could think of several ways to commit suicide in a shower--*hanging yourself from a shower rod, electrocution, drowning, scalding,* I supposed. *I don't need to be in a place like this, I just wanted some damned sleep.*

I threw the tattered robe over me and turned the odd, knobless handle that latched our door. *Doorknobs could also help you kill yourself?* That was harder to think of. *Maybe just hanging? Or smashing your face in with it.*

Across the hallway, the Community Room door was open. That meant it had to be at least 5AM. That's what the paperwork from the night before had said anyway. A man and a woman sat inside at a table. They both appeared to be about 60, naturally, they both had on outfits that matched mine. I recognized the man's long gray beard right away. The man playing cards last night. It wasn't a hallucination.

The woman cradled a styrofoam cup. I sat on a chair right by the door, as far away from these crazy people as I could.

"Hey," she said with a smoker's husk. "You new?"

"Yeah," I replied, "how do you take a shower here?"

"Sorry, Honey. They don't open til 10 and there'll be a wait list today. 4th of July gets all the vets. It's gonna be a madhouse."

The man waved his hand and chuckled "I come back here every year. They save a bed for me."

"I'm sorry," I said.

"I'm not!" the woman chuckled "I'm getting out today. Psych said so."

"You lying fucking whore!" the man retorted "You've been saying that for 4 days. Psych's not even in on Sundays!"

The woman laughed.

"Hey." I interrupted them, "I need to see a doctor. Did you just say he's out on Sundays? I just had a baby. I just need to be prescribed something to sleep so I can get back to him–"

A nurse in tie-dyed scrubs wheeled into a portable nurse station. "Meds!" she announced. "And…" she bent down to the middle shelf of her station. "Cake for breakfast!" She explained further as she set out two unopened boxes of sheet cake at the center table of the Community Room, "The main hospital cafeteria had some leftover sheet cakes from the 4th of July, so they sent them over to us. Turns out, not many people order a cake for their rooms during a pandemic. Surprise, surprise. Ah well, more for us."

"Cecil first," she said, beeping something to open a medicine box. "Have you been out of the country in the last two weeks?"

"You know damn well I been in here for the past two weeks!"

More patients trickled into the cafeteria. They served themselves cups of water from the machine or grabbed crayons and started to color on printer paper. *This is really a crazy house.* I thought. I decided to move in from the door, only to claim a chair at a table before it got too crowded.

A patient in his early 40s took a seat next to me. He had kind dark eyes and ears that reminded me of Dopey from Snow White, and he smelled like musky balls. *At least we all stank.*

"Hi," he said in a measured tone. "I'm Joseph."

"I'm Rhonwyn," I said.

"Hi, Rhonwyn." He repeated slowly. *Was this an Al-Anon Meeting?*

"How are you feeling?" he asked. He was awkwardly serving himself some cake with a plastic spoon. No knives. *Stabbing.* That's an obvious one.

"Been better. I just had a baby."

"Congratulations. I'm sorry you're here."

"I'm sorry *you're* here," I echoed. I figured it was the polite thing to say. "Hey, is there any chance to see the Psych today?"

"No, he's out on Sundays. It's a minimum 72-hour hold anyway. Don't hold your breath." *Suffocation.* I guess that's one they can't stop.

I didn't reply.

"At least there's cake?" he joked.

I picked up a spoon and served myself a red white and blue cake. The stale sugar icing cracked with each impact of my spoon. Sheet cake. Stale sheet cake. Industrial-grade imitation vanilla extract flavor. Leftover from the night before. Bon Appetit.

"At least there's cake," I replied.

Joseph smiled.

"How long have you been in here?" I asked my new friend. The only way out was *through.*

Cake Pop! - A Notification

9 months in my belly, 9 months out. Postpartum was hard. You don't just bounce back from a grippy sock vacation. Especially waking up twice a night to feed and rock your infant. But by the spring of 2021, Jasper and I were well into a routine, and the fog was starting to clear (read: Lexapro kicked in).

Even better news was I was still working from home due to the pandemic. That meant that on Thursdays, Jasper and I had time to go to the local YMCA for infant swim class before I dropped him off at the recently-reopened daycare. Let me tell you; this boy was a fish. He lit up in the water, all splashes and giggles as the teenage swim instructors tried to piece together some semblance of a lesson plan for him and his classmates.

It was the last day of our six-week course. I was wrapping Jasper up in a T-Rex towel when Lifeguard McKenna approached us with a half strip of paper.

"I hope you can make it again next term!" she said with her low voice that always seemed far too deep for her bubbly persona. The first page was re-enrollment information for next term. On the back was a break-down of Jasper's swim performance of the period.

JASPER JURESTOVSKY SWIM REPORT CARD

- Water Comfort: 5/5
- Leg Kicks: 2/5
- Ability to Pull Out of Pool: 0/5
- Jumps into Pool: 0/5

Recommendation: Repeat Intro to Swim

I smiled at the paper - this would be going on the fridge. I didn't sign up looking to teach Jasper to swim. I was there for an exercise routine for myself. Lifting up 19 pounds of baby in and out of the water was no small feat, and he loved it! Still, I thought the report card was hilarious.

"Look buddy," I said, handing Jasper the report card, "Here's all of the games we practiced in the pool! Do we want to sign up again?"

The baby grabbed onto the paper, and drew it toward his mouth. He was cutting another tooth, and desperate for relief with any object he could get his hands on.

"Next period, we're moving to the same time Mondays! We hope you and Jasper can make it!" McKenna said as she dabbed at her red curls with the towel.

"I sure hope so," I told her, "we love it!"

After drying off, Jasper and I bundled up for the chilly spring weather. It was still in the mid-50s most weeks. I placed the re-enrollment paper on the passenger seat, and adjusted the mirror to look at my swim class graduate, who was strapped into his rear-facing car seat. His eyes were already heavy.

"It's still only 8:15 - Do you think we can swing by Starbucks to get mommy some caffeine before Daycare?"

"Gooo-gee Baa-doo!" Jasper babbled back.

I took it as a yes. We didn't do it every week, but the last week of classes felt momentous. I opened up the Starbucks App;

ADDED TO CART:
One (1) Grande Hot Vanilla Latte with Caramel Drizzle

"Jasper" I glanced back up through the mirrors. He opened his eyes, but didn't move a muscle. "Fun fact that I learned long ago; a "Caramel Macchiato" at Starbucks just means that they put the espresso in last. Otherwise, it's an overpriced Vanilla Latte. Order a Vanilla Latte with Caramel Drizzle, and you pay less for the exact same coffee. You're going to have to learn these things."

His eyes closed again. My fun facts were working, boring him to sleep.

I looked back at the app for my order. A notification popped up before it brought me to the cart.

STARBUCKS: They're Back! Spring into refreshment with our Zesty Lemon Cake Pops.

Oh, sure, I thought, *why not have a post-workout treat?* I took the upsell and added it to my order.

Cake pops—if you aren't familiar with the Pinterest trend of 2011 that just couldn't quit— are just ground-up sponge cakes mixed with icing. Roll the mixture up into a ball and plop it onto a stick. Then, for the shell, dip the stick into white chocolate. Voila - Pop! Of course, Starbucks employees don't have to do all that – I'm sure they do in the warehouses, but at your local store, the employees take the frozen pops out of the freezer on closing shift so they're thawed for the morning.

Cake pops. They're simple and accessible. At any given moment, I candrive up to the Starbucks on Hudson and Graham and grab a cake *pop for $2.79. I can even order it on an upsell from an app on a whim for a post-workout treat. I can decide if I'm going to have cake any time I please.* So that's exactly what I did.

* * *

The Starbucks on the corner of Hudson and Graham is horribly placed. The parking lot has an entrance coming in from both sides of the street, so when the line gets long, cars wrap around the building, blocking the Hudson entrance completely. This was a non-issue until the pandemic hit and drive-thru was the only option. Even if you placed your order in advance, you had to pick it up in the drive-thru.

I pulled into the Starbucks from Graham Rd, as is customary for this particular Starbucks location. Locals simply pretend the Hudson entrance didn't exist. It's better for the flow of traffic.

I pulled my car behind a red SUV, and put it in park. I glanced back at Jasper in the mirror. He was out like a light. Excellent.

Then–it happened...

Moving my gaze from the mirror to my front windshield, I saw a tiny white Sedan having the AUDACITY to pull into the Starbucks line from *Hudson Ave.*

Hudson! Can you believe it? I told you, this was not the custom at the Starbucks on Hudson and Graham. You pretend the Hudson entrance doesn't exist! That's the *rule*.

My eyes widened. I felt a cold sweat start to form–was this driver about to *cut in the line*?

I looked to the red SUV in front of me–the Sedan's potential line-cutting victim.

Luckily, with Jasper napping, he would not be witness to such injustice.

The SUV let off her brakes inching forward to lay claim to her rightful position. Despite clearly being able to see us, the driver of the Sedan responded in turn taking a foot off the break to inch forward.

This was Minotaur vs. Theseus. Hamilton vs. Burr. Mr. Prosperi vs. That Family that Cut in Line at Journey to Bethlehem. Worse yet, if this red SUV won, I was next up to battle.

Bright red lights came on from the car ahead of me in line. Brake lights. The SUV surrendered.

The driver of the Sedan inched forward, waving the awkward hand symbol of "whoops I fucked up."

The rest of the line went smoothly, but my eyes shot daggers at the back of the white Sedan as she pulled into her order. This white Sedan was now putting an extra 8.5 feet between me and my cake pop. I don't take kindly to people who get between me and my cake. I'm sure you've noticed by this point in the book, but I really ... really ... *really* like cake.

I laughed to myself, loopy from the silly battle I just witnessed. It was nice to find humor in the every day again. I was feeling more and more like the old me.

I opened my phone to scroll through TikTok while I waited in the drive-thru. It was only 8:24, so I wouldn't be late with one extra car in front of me.

Algorithmically driven toddler videos crossed my screen. A man chasing his toddler with a diaper saying "Don't run from the Lord!" I chuckled. Then I swiped up. The Formula Mom was sharing her tips and solidarity on getting past the #BreastIsBest judgment; I nodded in agreement and swiped up again.

Buzz! - An email interrupted my scrolling. It was from HR.

HR@obphic.com - **Subj.** Return to Office Plan

"Fuck," I cursed aloud. *Goodbye, Swim Class.*

Jasper's First Cake

June 2021 meant Jasper made it one trip around the sun! My little boy was turning one year old. With the pandemic numbers dropping, that also meant we could have grandparents from both sides join the celebration! What better way to celebrate the occasion than with a smash cake? A chance to bequeath my sweet tooth to the next generation. A true rite of passage!

One problem; Jasper wasn't into solids yet.

My 11.5-month-old was just about the worst eater out there. With this kid, it was purees, formula, or bust. The pediatrician said not to be too concerned. Of course, me being me, I *was* concerned. I worry – that's what I do best. I worried that Jasper wasn't eating enough and he'd starve to death—yes, this was a real worry despite him being THE chunkiest one-year-old at daycare. I worried he'd be malnourished, so his teeth wouldn't grow right. I worried that the motor delays meant he had some kind of larger undetected cognitive issue.

Albeit a smaller worry, I worried about his cake. I worried he would be missing out if he didn't enjoy a cake on his first birthday.

This is why I decided Jasper would have two birthday cakes for his party. Yep! TWO!

The first of the two would be a tiny strawberry-banana-flavored smash cake.

You know Smash Cakes, don't you? Really they can be any flavor, but the goal of a smash cake is to load it up with some kind of whipped icing. This way when the 1-year-old smashes their fingers into it, you can have an adorable mess for the camera. Alternatively, you have a trepidatious kid who sticks one finger in the whipped icing and recoils in fear. Either way, smash cakes are camera-ready. Strawberry and banana were the only two flavors I had any luck with him eating, so why wouldn't it work in a cake?

The second was your classic run-of-the-mill chocolate cake. Needs no introduction - where could that go wrong? Jasper was bound to like one of them, right? *Right??*

I bought the ingredients the week before his birthday, to make the cakes one of the days that week after work, in time for the Saturday party. Wishful thinking; between returning to the OBPHiC office 3 days a week, and the constant stream of communications we had to pass on to ticket buyers because of the changes in COVID statuses, I was glued to either my computer or phone from sunup to sundown.

By the time his party rolled around, there were no cakes to be shown for it. I reassured myself it would be okay. Derek's mom and my parents could entertain the kid while I could bake away in the kitchen. That was the plan anyway. The day finally arrived! Jasper was overjoyed to see his grandparents, and I got to work on my dualling cakes.

Alright, I narrated to myself after assessing the kitchen, *Smash Cake First.*

I pulled out my mixing bowls to pour in the ingredients. Flour, baking powder, and freeze-dried strawberries into one. Jasper helped with that part; hearing me pound the freeze-dried strawberries into a powder piqued his curiosity, so he crawled in to help. He happily covered himself in flour while I mixed the wet ingredients; bananas, eggs, milk, and sugar. I smiled at my baking assistant who was coated in powder on the floor. It was a glimpse into our future baking together, I just knew it.

But then my phone buzzed. A streak of batter smeared the screen as I opened the email; a baking hazard that has followed me through many phones in my lifetime.

From: Natalie George
Subject: FWD: American Cast Only for the Edinburgh Women's Choir

Hey Rhonwyn,
There was a positive COVID test in the European cast, so at least 8 members have to be replaced. We have to take down any collateral with the European cast's faces on it. We need this done now if we're going to get it in time for donor pre-sale. Thank you!

–Nat

Ugh - I wiped my fingers off unsuccessfully to start my replies. The Edinburgh Women's Choir was going to be our first show since COVID closed the theaters, we couldn't have this pre-sale go wrong. My coordinator and I were in charge of the landing page, email, and social media, so we had our work cut out for us. Batter smeared all over my phone screen as I tapped away shooting out various emails and texts.

From: Rhonwyn Crownover
To: Lori Phillips, Bethany Couch
Subject: FWD: American Cast Only for the Edinburgh Women's Choir

Hey Lori,

Rhonwyn from OBPHiC here — we just received word that the European cast is no longer going to make it to Cleveland. Can you please create web sizes for the graphic using this attached logo only?

I apologize for the short notice.

-Rhonwyn

I flipped open my text tab to reach out to Bethany, the social media coordinator.

BETHANY

Hey girl!
I'm SOOO sorry, just forwarded you an email
from Matt & Nat. They're swapping out to the American
cast officially, so you have to make sure your posts
this weekend don't have any of that cast on there. I'd
do logo-only just in case they change their mind for the
third time. You know how it's been lately. ☹

Grazie!

UGHHHHH

I'm literally at Cedar Point today.
☺ LOLOL

... Do we have a logo-only picture?

Sorry. It's the worst.

Yes. Lori's getting you a new pic now.

Got it. I'll just cancel today's for now
and wait for Lori's stuff.

Perrrfect, thanks! 😀 😀 😀

😀 😀 😀

BEEEEEEEEEEEEEEEEEEEEEP!

The blast of the oven's alert brought me back to the task in front of me. *Right,* I thought, *the oven was preheating.* Our freakishly-fast gas stove was not conducive to working and baking at the same time.

I quickly poured the dry mixture in with the wets before schlepping them into the baking pans. The cake was baking, the work fire was put out and I could go back to my regularly scheduled celebration.

The rest of the family was in the living room with Jasper. Derek was holding Jasper while he pounded down a bottle of formula. I sat down to join them.

"How about some presents?!" my dad asked, bringing out a color-fully wrapped box that I knew contained his very first toddler trike.

Jasper screamed with excitement as he ripped open more presents from relatives that COVID prevented him from meeting. A basket-ball hoop from Derek's mom, a water table from my Nana, and a toy Recycling Truck from his aunts. We Zoomed with anyone we could answer so they could join in the fun.

BEEEEEEEEEEEEEEEEEEEP!

40 minutes in, the oven beeped again. I grabbed my phone off the kitchen counter to see where Lori was at with the design. Already finished–speedy as always.

While the cake cooled, I loaded up Lori's new images of Edinburgh Women's Choir onto the website. All was well, now when the subscribers got the email this afternoon, there would be no trace of Edinburgh's actual residents for our new American-only choir.

I paused. *There's a marketing email going out today.* I had social media covered with Bethany, and I swapped the website but I forgot about the email that was scheduled to go out this afternoon.

My laptop was still on the kitchen table from my work earlier that morning. I opened a browser to our CRM, my heart was pounding to the beat of the rotating circle on the loading screen. *Was the email set for 10 or 11? It's 10:55, best case scenario I'm at the skin of my teeth.* I clicked through to my email blast.

> "OBPHiC Welcomes Edinburgh Women's Choir - Tickets on Sale Tomorrow!"
> *– Scheduled for 11:00 AM*
>
> *SEND NOW | EDIT | DUPLICATE | CANCEL*

Oh, thank God. I sighed with relief as I tapped the EDIT button.

I opened it up, quickly replacing the information for the Edinburgh Women's Choir show, and updating it with the new logo from Lori. For good measure, I rescheduled it for noon.

Phew. Natalie would have been pissed if I missed that. I shut my laptop for a moment.

Oh Right, Icing.
Store-bought icing was enough for the cake. I decorated the green icing and stuck a blue sparkly "1" candle on top. I had a bit of banana left, so I cut it into four slices and put them at the bottom of the little cake. It was reminiscent of, but in no way resembled a car–I figured he'd like it.

"Happy Birthday to you!..." I sang as I re-entered the party with the candle.

My mom lifted Jasper onto his high chair in front of the balloons we'd put out for him. My rolly polly baby eyed the bright flame on the cake I was holding. I kept at a distance.

"...Happy Birthday to you!" The family chimed in.

'Happy Birthday dear Jasper

Happy Birthday to you!"

"Hooray!" we all cheered

Jasper looked terrified to see all the grown-ups clapping and singing in unison. We laughed at how weird of an experience that must have been for him.

"Want to blow out the candle, Peanut?" Derek's mom asked as she pointed toward the cake.

Jasper looked at the cake but just played with his hands apprehensively. I laughed and blew out the candle. Smoke swirled upward from the candle. "Coud!" Jasper said, pointing at the rising smoke. "That's right, a little cloud!" I said to him.

We all cood over the little boy as he grazed an index finger against his cool whip icing, getting just a tiny smear of it on his finger. Jasper brought the bit of icing to his mouth for a test. His eyes widened as the sweet silky flavor reached his mouth.

"Is that yummy?" I asked him, excited.

Jasper took more and more licks of icing and even dipped one of the banana slices into it to suck on. He wasn't ready for the sponge.

The grownups chatted as Jasper picked away at his cake, eventually lifting the plate up, causing the cake to drop onto the floor, icing side down. Ah well, that's how it goes. I picked the bulk of the cake up, but Virginia darted toward the spill, lapping at the icing.

"Kitty, no!" I scolded. She scurried back into her room. She had a history of messing with my cakes, and I wasn't about to chance it.

My mom picked Jasper up, and she left with his other grandma to the backyard to set up the new toy water table.

"Weren't we going to have chocolate cake?" Derek asked from the kitchen. He was bringing back a few sheets of paper towels for the cleanup.

"Oh shit, I forgot!" I looked at the time and it was already 11:45, pushing naptime for Jasper. "I was going to start it right after I pulled his banana one out, but then work had to swap all these images..."

"It's fine, I already started mixing it" Derek reassured me, "You go enjoy the party."

"Thanks, love"

"Mhmm"

Buzz.

Before I could even step outside, my phone buzzed again— Natalie. Text this time.

GROUP CHAT: MATT, NATAL...

Natalie: Hey everyone, I just emailed you, but this is urgent. Please cancel all EWC announcements today. We're postponing.

We want to try to get the Euro Cast back
but it means delaying the announcement.
Sorry for the chaos this weekend.

Matt: Hey Nat, the Announcement was for
11AM today. It's already been sent.

Rhonwyn: Actually, it hasn't gone out yet.
Plus since you said no faces, we removed the
cast in general so if it goes out, it doesn't
promise either cast, just generally says
the show is coming to OBPHIC.

Natalie: Ooooooh. That might work. Let me ask.

Natalie: Rhonwyn, standby. Matt, can you hop on
a meeting real quick to talk this through?

Natalie: Matt, when does the email go out?

Rhonwyn: Noon. But I can push to later.

Matt: Yeah I can hop on a meeting.

Natalie: Thank you. Rhonwyn standby.

I sighed to myself. "Standby." *Like I have nothing better to do than wait to see what the Women's Choir plans for their announcement in Ohio. For a show 3 months from now.*

GROUP CHAT: MATT, NATAL…

Me: *Standing by.*

I returned to the living room to find my little round toddler rubbing his eyes and eyeing the presents. He was getting sleepy. I scooped him up.

"Booh," he said, gesturing to the book that his Uncle Wes sent for his birthday. A car racing book.

"The vehicles rev their engines up." I read to Jasper, "5, 4, 3, 2, 1 - Off they go, they're on their way, the racing has begun! … "

The book counts down from 10 as each racecar gets stuck, lifted, or distracted from the race. Ice Cream Truck, Racer number 4 was just about to get stuck in desert cactus spines when I looked down at my little racer. Jasper was out, mouth wide open. *When did he get so big?*

I carried him into his crib, walking past family members who made sweet faces at the sleeping baby.

I set my little one-year-old into his crib, and held my breath, hoping I wouldn't wake him. He turned over without a peep. *Perfect transfer.*

By the time I got back out to the party, Derek had just finished serving up his chocolate cake to the grownups. He held out his plate to me as I settled in next to him on the couch. We always shared that kind of thing. I took a bite from the plastic fork. He'd done a great job finishing it up. I was grateful to him, but guilty that I couldn't finish it myself in time.

I listened to my dad, who was explaining his backyard project to Derek's mom – A patio that my parents built in their house in Arizona. My dad swiped through the pictures while my Mother-in-Law nodded.

"That's what toddler parties are," my mom said "Just a quick celebration, then the grownups just hang out while they nap."

I smiled and started to say something in agreement, but I was interrupted by the all-too-familiar buzz of my phone.

It was work.

No Cake October

I couldn't agree more; I've had plenty.

Step 5

Ice Your Cake

Thanks for the Lemon-cake

Five years, two houses, one pandemic, and one baby after our marriage, Derek was *finally* **graduating with his Ph.D.!** I took Thursday and Friday off of work to watch him walk and then get ready for the party. It was my first time taking vacation days from my new job. I put my phone on airplane mode. This was going to be different than before. A Ph.D. is a big deal. And for someone who never celebrated himself, I had to make sure he knew it.

We could spot Derek immediately as we found our own seats, even from 3 stories of bleachers up. He and his colleague Tim were just about the only two graduates wearing masks. Leave it to the two doctors of biology to keep their masks on; COVID was over, wasn't it?

"Look Jasper, it's Dada!" I pointed out to my almost two-year-old. He didn't understand.

Instead, he looked around to clap alongside the crowd as the University of Akron' President took the stage for his speech. It was your every day "Top Ten Tips to Succeed in the Real World" formula. Four about work, three about kindness, two about friendship, and one cringey dad joke.

Jasper started asking "Mama, down?" Around the time of the Akron President's Tip #7, in which he explained that "You can always depend on people who own house cats" (Insert polite laughter here). I slid the wiggly toddler off my lap so he could ham it up in the front aisle.

"Mama, jwump!" Jasper pleaded. To make a point, he extended his arms behind himself to generate the force needed for his extreme jumping. He was the star of the show until the graduates arrived.

The crowd erupted in applause. No doubt because Jasper actually got some air underneath his Dinosaur Sneakers with that last jump. The Akron University President stepped off stage.

As Ph.D. students, Derek and his cohort got to walk first. I scooped Jasper up to get a better look at the stage.

We clapped politely through the alphabet, adding a quick "Woo!" of excitement for Derek's friend, Tim.

"Derek Joseph Jurestovsky," The announcer called, "Doctor of Philosophy in Integrated Bioscience. Dissertation: Snake Biomechanics and Locomotion."

"YAAAAY DADAAAA" I shouted, hoping he could hear me. Jasper looked around him to see where Dada was.

I returned to my seat to meet up with my in-laws. They were already packing up to head out of the stadium—as moms themselves, they know how these kinds of things work with a toddler.

I handed Jasper to my sister-in-law who couldn't get enough baby snuggles that weekend. "Did Twuck!" Jasper pointed to the parked Zamboni. "Big Truck?" I translated, "That does look like a truck, doesn't it?"

I put my own arm around Diane. "Are you proud of your boy?" I asked. The white-haired woman's face was drenched with tears. She nodded, unable to say a word. I gave her a quick hug. My own eyes were welling up.

* * *

We drove to the party after pictures and lunch. My parents had already arrived at the rental lodge with all the food we'd ordered. I inspected the large pink box in the center of the food table.

Derek's cake was a white sheet cake with purple and pink balloons on it. I'd only ordered it that same morning, so my options were limited. In purple icing was the script "Doctorate Denied" A Futurama quote turned inside-joke for the Doctoral candidates as they made their way through the last few years. He was gonna love it.

"BEEPA!" Jasper squealed with delight at the sight of my dad.

"JASPER!" My dad greeted his grandson with a big hug.

Congratulations and celebrations continued throughout the evening as guests ate and chatted. Jasper and his Grandpa chased each other up and down the hall of the lodge.

Absent-mindedly, I wandered to the couches by the lodge fireplace and checked my phone.

NOTIFICATIONS: 1

Amber: Hey we're running late to the party. Be there at 6...

It was already past 6, so Amber and Thibaut had already arrived. I marked her text as read, and refreshed my Messages, Email, and Slack. *Nothing*.

I wondered what I was expecting. This was the first vacation day I'd taken at my new job. I turned my notifications off, but that had never worked at OBPHiC. They'd just... text anyway because it was urgent. *Was it actually going to be a vacation day?*

"Bid twuck!!!!" Jasper exclaimed, running to the window to watch a semi-truck drive past.

"Big truck! That's right" Derek repeated back.

I took in the scene. My parents chatted away with my in-laws in the seating area. Our friends were gathered on the right side of the table, laughing and drinking with Derek. This was the first time friends and family of ours were all in one place since the pandemic began. My pandemic toddler ran back and forth between them. He continued pointing out his toys to everyone he recognized.

I rejoined the party, forgetting my phone on the side of my seat.

"Who's ready for cake?" I asked. Derek to cheese it up as he cut into his "Doctorate Denied" birthday cake.

Jasper got the first piece. He poked a single finger into the icing and inspected his hand. Maybe next time.

The party guests and family thinned two-by-two, each contributing to the cleanup efforts. My parents took Jasper back to the house for bed.

Soon the lodge was empty except for Derek and me. I was calm, serene even. I thought of the European cathedrals we'd explored on our honeymoon. Derek's footsteps echoed as he anxiously walked the lodge kitchen to make absolutely sure we weren't forgetting anything.

I set my own bags down on the table under the EXIT sign, freeing up a hand to search for "Chris Rice" on YouTube.

"So go ahead and ask her..." Our wedding song began to echo through the quiet lodge.

Derek smiled at me from the kitchen.

"...for Happy Ever After. 'Cause nobody knows what's coming, so why not take a chance on loving?... "

Without saying a word, we met each other in the middle of the room. He took me in his arms to dance to our wedding song–the only song we ever dance to (outside of Quelf).

As the song finished, Derek took my face in his hands and pulled me in for a kiss. I could still taste a faint trace of sweet buttercream icing on his lips.

Thank you to;

My mom, who taught me how to bake Cake.

My dad, who taught me how to eat Cake.

My husband, Derek, who gave me the confidence to share my recipes.

To [NAME REDACTED], who didn't give me cake, which, in many ways, gave me Cake.

Danielle Hevey, Alec Kozak, Austin Lanser, Kristen Poulos, and Amber Rayl, who licked the batter from the spoon.

My secret ingredients, who appear as characters and composites in this story. You have all impacted my life in a very real way.

My not-so-secret ingredients, who let me use your real names in this story. I'm equally grateful to, and humbled by each of you. Much like those fondant cake-toppers, my depictions don't do a drop of justice to your true selves.

Finally, thank you to my son Jasper, to whom I dedicate this book. You've taught me that there are more important things to life than Cake.

BAKE SALE!

I want to hear *your* stories. Follow me on Instagram at @rhonwrites, then share your share your favorite cake memory with the hashtag #ihopeyoulikecake.

www.ingramcontent.com/pod-product-compliance
Lightning Source LLC
Chambersburg PA
CBHW050329160726
48002CB00001B/243